Tend Your Garden

90 Days to a Life of Purpose

Wes Feltner Ph.D.
& Lance Tanaka

Tend Your Garden

90 Days to a Life of Purpose

Wes Feltner Ph.D. & Lance Tanaka

ISBN (Print Edition): 978-1-09831-555-9

ISBN (eBook Edition): 978-1-09831-556-6

Table of Contents

Preface: Created For Purpose   1

Introduction: Transformation Stories   3

Part One: Welcome to the Garden   11

What is your Garden?   13

Your Personal Garden Tools   17

Don't Look for the "Answer"   29

**Part Two: Using the Dream and Achieve
(DNA) Method to Plant Your Seeds**   37

STEP 1 – Identify Your DNA® ELEMENTS   39

Identify Your Passions   39

Identify Your Strengths   47

STEP 2 - DNA® DRILL DOWN   54

Find Your Elements   54

STEP 3 - DNA® ACTION   71

Small Steps Are Key   71

Develop New Habits   85

Move Down the Path   97

It's a Process   101

Testimonials   108

References   111

About the authors   114

Preface: Created For Purpose

Many of us want to know there is a reason why we are here on this earth. We need to believe we have a purpose beyond our daily work and toil. We yearn to hear the voice of God or see the writing in the sky that will explain our mission, our purpose, and the path to achieving it. There is a simple reason for this: we were created *on purpose* and *for purpose*. Purpose is built within the DNA of every human being. It was God's design from the very beginning.

We all want to be happy—to have a fulfilling, purpose-driven, God inspired career; to have healthy, happy, loving relationships; to be financially secure, etc. But happiness can elude us. We often don't see our purpose. We may lack a direction. We may know our dream but feel it's too far away to achieve. Many of us don't know how to take the first steps. We are waiting for that voice, that sign from on high.

Waiting can lead to drifting, and drifting leads to a life lived without purpose.

The truth is that most of us will never hear a booming voice in the sky. We'll never get that clear sign that says, "Do this. Now!" But what if that's not a bad thing? What if God doesn't speak from the sky because he has already given you the answer?

We believe it is a question of knowing how to listen. If we listen to our own being, we find there is another way that the Lord speaks directly to each and every one of us: through our gifting.

That's right. Your natural gifts and abilities are the mark of God in you, nudging you toward the life path that will give you the greatest fulfillment, purpose, and, yes, happiness.

In this book, which accompanies the course of the same name, we want to help you discover and develop your innate gifting. *Tend Your Garden* uses the

Dream and Achieve® (DNA) process, a method developed by Lance Tanaka that has helped thousands of people overcome their purposelessness by:

- identifying their strengths and passions,

- developing practical action plans with effective steps they can take immediately, and

- building a discipline to do what needs to be done.

Let this book, in conjunction with the course and our DNA® certified coaches, walk you through this most important process. It is *our* passion to help you to identify your gifting so you can tend your garden, glorify God, and experience something amazing.

Introduction: Transformation Stories

We want to take you on a journey of transformation, a journey we and many others have gone on. Along the way, we will share many stories of discovery and growth.

What Transformation Looks Like

Before we do that, however, we want to introduce a framework we use to conceptualize transformation in our lives. While everyone's journey will be unique to them, the process itself tends to follow a predictable pattern:

Nudge

Something triggers us. Maybe it's the realization that we are not doing something of value. We don't feel fulfilled, we're not making a difference, we don't truly enjoy our work. It might be a situation where we see someone who loves what they are doing and are excited about the journey they're on and we envy them or feel dissatisfaction with our own lives. Maybe it's a life changing event that rattles our brain or heart.

One way or another, something nudges you to want to change. In other words, you're finally ready to do what you were designed to do.

Discovery

We begin the journey through prayer, talking with people, and identifying who we are—our strengths, passions, experiences, that is, our gifting. This can take place over a series of events and a long time. You may experience excitement, uncertainty, fear, confusion, all of which are normal as you start to transition into this new discovery.

Actions

Once we start understanding our gifts, we take small steps along our path-to-purpose. Each small action leads to more clarity and to subsequent next steps, moving us down the path.

Living God's Plan

Our objective is to define the elements of our dream, mission, purpose, and vision so we can be living in God's plan for our life. This is where true satis-faction is experienced. This is where God's blessings are enjoyed.

Typical Transformations

After doing thousands of DNA® exercises with people, we've discovered that people tend to experience one of three kinds of transformation:

Minor Course Correction

This is the most typical outcome for the DNA® process. People stay put in their personal lives and career but make adjustments that help them live into their gifts where they already are.

Your journey down the path-to-purpose doesn't need to upend your whole life. In one sense, it is simply a process of pushing out (deleting, delaying, deferring, diminishing) the things that run contrary to your gifting and pulling in things that are aligned—and doing this on a consistent, gradual basis. Although people around won't see the changes, over time they add up to a material transformation.

Examples of Minor Course Corrections

A manager in a Big 4 accounting firm realized she needed to work with other partners in the firm in order to expand her network. So, she started introducing herself to a small, select list of partners she admired to let them know she was available to assist them on their work. Over time, they started giving her assignments, thus expanding her reach.

A senior pastor of a church desired to spend more time with people and preparing for weekend sermons but found himself spending most of his time in administrative meetings and putting out fires around the office. When he realized how unhappy this made him, he hired an associate pastor to run the church and rewrote his own job description to allow him to focus on the things God gifted him to do.

An entrepreneur was nudged into integrating his Sunday spirituality into his Monday through Saturday work life. He set a target to read a chapter in the New Testament on a daily basis for one year.

A finance director sought out and volunteered for special projects that had nothing to do with his current job but were higher profile initiatives in his area of interests.

A Principal in a Big 3 consulting firm had to address his anger problems caused by stress. He decided to forge a habit of running. After a few successful months, he made a habit of running three times per week. It is now a lifestyle change for him.

After an analysis of why she was unhappy in her job, a Big 3 consultant decided to stop traveling on Sunday nights. This had a major impact on her family life.

All these people went through a discovery process to identify key elements needed in their life, took small steps which further clarified their elements that led to additional steps, and moved down the path-to-purpose. As they followed the process, they went through a life-altering mindset shift. They saw their prayers being answered, and they felt the joy of living a more pur-poseful life.

Sideways Shift Within Same Company/Industry

Many people discover that their current employer provides great opportu-nities for them to shift their role or emphasis in ways that better leverage their gifts and make more impact. In other words, sometimes you have found the right industry or field but are not in the best role to feel challenged and satisfied.

Examples of Sideways Shifts

Darren Ho, the Director of Sales/Marketing in Eli Lilly, used this platform to move into a passion for him: coaching. The company happened to be focus-ing on creating a coaching culture, so he applied and became the Director of Leadership and Employee Development of China, then rolled out a successful pilot which in turn catapulted him to a global role.

Kevin Gao, Head of Manufacturing for Baxter China, wanted to expand his horizons beyond China. Although there were opportunities outside, he realized Baxter gave him the platform he desired. After going through the discovery process, he took the needed small steps to get to the Head of Asia Pacific Manufacturing.

A Big 3 consulting firm principal was suffering poor results in the healthcare sector. This led him to question if the firm was the right place to be. After identifying his elements, he took the small steps of moving to the tech sector, networking with key partners, and building a business case for the value he could add.

A senior pastor realized that all the time spent preparing for sermons and ministering to people was draining him. He discovered he was more gifted in the area of finance and strategic planning, so he approached other leaders in the church and suggested that he change seats. He encouraged the church to find a new senior pastor so that he could focus on the areas that would better edify the church.

A life insurance executive changed his focus on where he wanted to have an impact, from Greater China to his home country of Singapore. While it was a difficult transition at first, over time it became a major stepping-stone to his next career.

Change of Vocation

This kind of transformation is the most difficult one to make. Before deciding to make a leap of faith, many have to process the feeling that changing vocations means they have wasted their years in their current vocation. This, however, is a mistake in thinking. It's the experience they've accumulated over the years that has put them into a position of purpose.

Lance's Story: A Change of Vocation

My (Lance's) own story is a good example of this last and most dramatic type of transformation. At any rate, if we expect you to be vulnerable enough to open yourself to transformation, the least we can do is share our own journeys. My transformation was a major one in terms of career but not so large in terms of my passions.

Nudge

At 35, I had already become an executive at Pepsico in Tokyo. The ride up the corporate ladder was wild and fast, and I was blessed by the opportunity, but there was something missing. I knew in my heart of hearts this role wasn't my destiny.

Then I read Stephen Covey's *First Things First*. He taught me that we must identify and act on the things in our life that are important even if they do not feel urgent—for example, health, relationships, and our life and career dreams. It was the nudge I needed.

Discovery

I began to take any assessment tool I could find to learn more about myself. These tools were good in that they helped me to expose my strengths and passions, but they all fell short in practical application. I wanted a tool or process that would help me to identify more specifically my gifts so that I could make a real change. In the middle of my self-discovery process, I began to put together the principles for what would become the Dream and Achieve® (DNA) method.

Three years into the period of my self-discovery, my wife and I met a couple at a party who invited us to their church. The pastor at the church was a Biblical scholar who ignited my desire to understand the intellectual side of the Christian story. This invitation proved to be another nudge—a divine one—and it led me to want to integrate my emotional and intellectual self with my faith. It led me to want to marry my faith in Jesus with my entrepreneurial gifting.

Actions

Through the process of learning more about myself, I discovered a critical secret: It's not the big changes or moves that make a difference, it's the little things over time that add up. It was a gradual process of pushing out the things that ran contrary to my strengths and passions and pulling in the things I was good at and loved doing.

"Don't worry about the money, worry about the people."

Living God's Plan

I eventually made the big jump to entrepreneurialism, starting up my own coaching/consulting firm. In the first year, I had not secured any significant clients and therefore was continually calculating the amount of money I could charge for any potential client. I was constantly worrying about the money. It was at this low point that I heard the Lord's crystal-clear message. "Don't worry about the money, worry about the people." This whack across the head is what I needed to hear. I immediately changed my mindset, stopped calculating, and focused on how I could impact people. Within a few days, two large clients signed up. I was on the road to fulfillment through integrating my spiritual and vocational lives.

How to use this book

This book is be used as a manual for the Tend Your Garden program. Your certified coach will walk you through the whole process and the 3 Steps along the way. While it is possible to work through the ideas and exercises yourself, going through the course and working with a coach provides you feedback and one-on-one attention and accountability that can accelerate your transformation.

Benefits of using a certified DNA® coach

This life/career critical process requires at times deep introspection. Your coach can help you by:

- asking the right questions
- providing guidance and examples of others who have gone through the process
- helping you break through some barriers
- keeping you on track

If you would like to find a DNA® certified coach, you can sign up for one at www.tendyourgarden.net.

The Dream and Achieve® (DNA) 3-step Process

In order to go through the process, you must use the Dream and Achieve® (DNA) Workbook. Each chapter has an accompanying exercise in the workbook. In the workbook you'll find:

- Worksheets for each of the 3 Steps of the DNA Process

- The MBTAM worksheet for developing new habits

- The Career Choice Guide

- Examples for completing each exercise

Go to www.tendyourgarden.net or www.lancetanakagroup.com to download your free copy. Requires MS Excel or similar spreadsheet program.

Terminology

Throughout the book, we use two terms interchangeably: *gifts* and *elements*. Quite simply, they mean the same thing.

The terms *career*, *work*, and *vocation* will also be used more or less synonymously, but they should be understood in an integrated sense alongside terms like *personal* or *home life*. This is because to truly live your gifting, your vocation and personal life must be integrated into your entire being. You need to use them extensively in your job, but you should also use them in your family life. They must be consistent. You shouldn't have one life on Sunday and a different one Monday through Saturday.

We also interchangeably use these four terms: dream, mission, purpose, and vision. Each is a way of speaking about God's plan for you.

When we refer to "we" it means both Wes and Lance. When we use the word "I," we will make it clear whether it is Lance or Wes speaking.

Part One:
Welcome to the Garden

What is your Garden?

Rethinking Paradise

Imagine a scenario where you could have anything you wanted, anytime you wanted it, and you didn't have to work to get it. Your favorite drink, favorite food, entertainment of choice—all right there at your fingertips. Sounds perfect, right? Maybe sounds a little like heaven!

If we are honest, when most of us think of Heaven or "paradise," we think of a reality removed from work: the endless vacation, the perfect retirement, or maybe just the weekend. Our typical way of thinking is that if we could somehow be free of work, life would be fulfilling and satisfying.

The truth is, this is backward thinking. It is the exact opposite of what we were created for.

In the opening chapters of Genesis, God creates humanity and places them in the Garden of Eden, and when God finishes putting all the pieces in place, He looks at it and calls it "very good." It's the ideal world; it is how things are intended to be.

You might expect, based on the way we usually think, that it would be a world without work or effort. And, truth be told, that's how we often think of Adam and Eve in the garden: lying around eating fruit, playing with animals, walking and talking with God, having their couple's devotional. It is all so spiritual and vacation-like, but that's not really the picture we get from Scripture:

> Then God said, "Let us make man in our image, after our likeness. And let them have dominion over the fish of the sea and over the birds of the heavens and over the livestock and over all the earth and over every creeping thing that creeps

on the earth." So God created man in his own image, in the image of God he created him; male and female he created them. (Genesis 1:26-27)

What does God do after creating humanity "in His image"? He gives them a job to do: "To exercise dominion over creation." Genesis 1:26-27 says humanity, male and female, were created "in God's image." Many people over the years have theorized that what it means to be created in God's image is that human beings are moral agents as God is a God of right and wrong, or that we are rational as God is rational, or even that we were created to be in relationships as God is a Triune God. All of these are true on their own, but they overlook what Scripture says specifically in the text: "let us create man in our image and let them have dominion over creation."

Part of bearing the image of God is to have dominion, that is to care for and work the Creation. After all, what has God been doing up until that point in Genesis? *Creating! Working!* God was not on vacation. He was not passive. He was acting, working, making things come into existence!

As we work, we worship

If we assume God was creating on purpose, we can infer that **He created humanity *with* purpose!** Human beings would image God in the world as they faithfully cultivated the world around them. Another way of saying that is as we work, we worship. This is at the very core of creation, what God intended for human beings to do from the beginning.

As the narrative of Scripture continues in Genesis, Adam and Eve's purpose takes on more concrete forms. They were not only called to have dominion over creation, but also to become one (marriage relationships), be fruitful and multiply (family relationships), steward their resources (take care of the things entrusted to them), and specifically "work their garden" (Genesis 2:15).

We take the garden as our central metaphor to capture this idea of being created to work as worship to God ("image bearing") by taking care of the resources, relationships, and all that we each have been entrusted with.

Personal Application

Before you continue reading, answer the following questions:

What is your current attitude towards your work or vocation?

_____

_____

_____

_____

_____

Do you find your work fulfilling and satisfying?

_____

_____

_____

_____

_____

What motivates in your current vocation?

_____

_____

_____

_____

_____

You Are Called to Work Your Garden

We believe that what happened with the first human beings is true for all human beings, namely, that **God has given you a garden to tend and work**

for His glory, and that in doing so you can experience satisfaction and fulfillment and do good in the world around you. It may be a nurse caring for a dying man, an entrepreneur starting a business, a musician writing a song, a scientist advancing medical research, a pastor preaching a sermon, a farmer providing crops to sustain a community, and so on. Everybody has a garden (purpose) wherein they image God (worship) by working and keeping it (vocation).

Not only do we believe that everyone has a garden to tend, but we also believe that you will never be truly satisfied until you discover what your garden is *and* start working it. Look at Genesis 2:

The Lord God took the man and put him in the garden of Eden to work it and keep it. And the Lord God commanded the man, saying, "You may surely eat of every tree of the garden…" (Genesis 2:15-16)

God tells Adam that his eating—from which he derived enjoyment, pleasure, and satisfaction—is directly related to his working (purpose, calling, vocation). In other words, God has created it so that when you discover your purpose (work the ground, expand the garden, etc.) you also enjoy great pleasure (eat and enjoy the fruit of your labor).

This doesn't mean that finding our purpose will be easy or be without struggle (after all in Genesis 3, sin enters the picture and disrupts the beautiful dance between purpose and pleasure), but it does mean our satisfaction in life is directly tied to discovering the purpose for which God has created us.

That is what this book is all about. We want to help you discover your garden. But we want to do more than to help you discover it, we want to give you the tools and direction to work it, grow it, and cultivate it not only for your good, but also for the good of the world and the glory of God. We do not want to just give you information; we want to compel you to action—action that will take you down the road of finding fulfillment in worshipping God with your whole life.

Your Personal Garden Tools

Instructions from Scripture: God Gives Us an Abundance of Gifts

Every night Julio Diaz would leave work, catch an hour-long subway ride to his neighborhood in the Bronx, and stop by his favorite diner. But one night this normal routine took a sudden twist. As Julio stepped of the #6 train onto the platform, a teenage boy approached with a knife and demanded his wallet. Julio, not wanting things to escalate, gave the boy his wallet.

As the boy turned to go away, Julio shouted, "Wait! If you're going to be robbing people tonight, you might as well take my coat to keep you warm." The robber stopped, turned and looked at Julio, who was holding out his jacket. As the boy reached for the jacket he asked, "Why are doing this?" Julio said, "If you're willing to risk your freedom for a few dollars, you must need the money. I was going to eat. If you'd like, you could join me."

To Julio's amazement, the boy agreed, and they went to Julio's favorite diner. The boy was amazed how Julio knew everyone. He was even nice to the man washing dishes.

The boy asked Julio, "Why are you so nice to people?"

Julio replied, "Haven't you been taught you should be nice to others?"

"Yes, but I didn't think people actually behaved that way."

The two continued in conversation for a few hours. Finally, the bill arrived. Julio said, "I'd be happy to pay for the meal, but you've got my wallet." The teenager gave Julio the wallet—along with the knife.

When Julio told his mother the story, she said, "Julio, you're the type of guy that if someone asked you for the time, you'd give them your watch."

Why do we love stories of generosity like this? Could it be because we're created in the image of an extravagantly generous God, a God who loves to be generous with His gifts?

That's exactly what we find in the pages of Scripture.

Remember back in the Garden? When God gave humanity life, He also gave them trees that were pleasant, then He gave them abundant food to eat and a river for nourishment. Then He gave them human companionship. In other words, from the beginning of creation God has been radically generous in His giving of gifts.

We see the same thing in the ministry of Jesus. Consider the Feeding of the Five Thousand:

> [Jesus] ordered the crowds to sit down on the grass, and taking the five loaves and the two fish, he looked up to heaven and said a blessing. Then he broke the loaves and gave them to the disciples, and the disciples gave them to the crowds. And they all ate and were satisfied. And they took up twelve baskets full of the broken pieces left over. (Matthew 14:19-20)

In this famous story, Jesus feeds a large crowd not with a little food but with an abundance of food. The baskets were running over in a culture that depended on "give us this day our daily bread."

Paul says to the Philippians that they can be confident that God will supply every need of yours according to his riches in glory in Christ Jesus (Philippians 4:19). To the Ephesians he writes, "But grace was given to each one of us according to the measure of Christ's gift. Therefore, it says, 'When he ascended on high he led a host of captives, and he gave gifts to men'" (Ephesians 4:7-8).

An entire book could be written on the generosity of God. God loves to give gifts, and these gifts come in a variety of forms: relationships, family, financial blessing, salvation, grace, talents or "spiritual gifts," even life itself. The gifts of God are abounding and fill our lives every day!

Scripture is not only clear on God's generosity in gift giving, but also His expectation to **use those gifts for His glory.** In a word: obedience! Remember, in the garden, Adam and Eve were to enjoy the gifts of God but at the same time not to eat of what was forbidden.

In 1 Timothy 4, Paul tells Timothy specifically, "do not neglect the gift within you." That is, you've been given a gift, don't ignore it, misuse it, or neglect it. It was given for you to use!

Point: God gives an abundance of gifts, and God expects us to enjoy and use those gifts in the garden He has entrusted to us.

You Must Use Your Gifts

It was a Friday morning, in the middle of rush hour at a Washington, D.C., metro station. A man emerged from the crowd and took a place against the wall. He had on blue jeans, a long-sleeve t-shirt, and a Washington Nationals baseball cap. He opened a small case, pulled out a violin, and over the next 43 minutes played six classical pieces. During that time, 1,100 people passed by. Most of them didn't even stop to listen for even a moment.

Had they stopped, they might have realized this wasn't any violinist; this was Joshua Bell, the internationally acclaimed violinist who three days earlier sold out Boston's Symphony Hall, with the cheapest seat going for $100. But on this day Joshua only received $30. Had they stopped, they might have also noticed he wasn't playing a pawnshop violin, but an 18th century violin worth over 3.5 million dollars. But on this day, Joshua and his violin could not grab the attention of busy people on their way to work.

An unbelievable opportunity was right in front of them, and they never even noticed. They never took advantage of it.

The truth is, we are all like those people in the subway that day. Surrounded by great opportunities, yet often never stopping to realize it. In the daily grind and routine of life we often neglect the specific things God has entrusted us with.

Jesus told a parable about this:

> For it will be like a man going on a journey, who called his servants and entrusted to them his property. To one he gave five talents, to another two, to another one, to each according to his ability. Then he went away.

> He who had received the five talents went at once and traded with them, and he made five talents more. So also he who had the two talents made two talents more. But he who had received the one talent went and dug in the ground and hid his master's money.

> Now after a long time the master of those servants came and settled accounts with them. And he who had received the five talents came forward, bringing five talents more, saying, "Master, you delivered to me five talents; here, I have made five talents more."

> His master said to him, "Well done, good and faithful servant. You have been faithful over a little; I will set you over much. Enter into the joy of your master."

> And he also who had the two talents came forward, saying, "Master, you delivered to me two talents; here, I have made two talents more."

> His master said to him, "Well done, good and faithful servant. You have been faithful over a little; I will set you over much. Enter into the joy of your master."

> He also who had received the one talent came forward, saying, "Master, I knew you to be a hard man, reaping where you did

not sow, and gathering where you scattered no seed, so I was afraid, and I went and hid your talent in the ground. Here, you have what is yours."

But his master answered him, "You wicked and slothful servant! You knew that I reap where I have not sown and gather where I scattered no seed? Then you ought to have invested my money with the bankers, and at my coming I should have received what was my own with interest. So take the talent from him and give it to him who has the ten talents. For to everyone who has will more be given, and he will have an abundance. But from the one who has not, even what he has will be taken away. And cast the worthless servant into the outer darkness. In that place there will be weeping and gnashing of teeth." (Matthew 25:14–30)

This story, known as the "Parable of the Talents," teaches us something about how we ought not neglect the gifts and opportunities given to us. In Jesus' day, it was a weight measure or portion of money equal to about six days' wages, but most scholars agree that the larger application represents more than monetary value. It represents the sum of all that God has entrusted us with. The point is simply that God has graciously given us more than we deserve—and we should faithfully use what the master has given us!

Practical Application

Stop, here, and make a list of all the different opportunities God has graciously given you:

_____

_____

_____

_____

_____

Responding to Your Gift

The heart of this story isn't just what the servants were given but what they did with their gifts. Notice the different responses. The first two servants—we might call them the Diligent Servants—go to work immediately. They are prompt, active, and efficient. They don't spend hours on Facebook, playing computer games, doodling on paper while the clock was ticking. They take what they've been entrusted with seriously. The text says they "invested" it, that is, put it to work or made it grow.

What also stands out about the second servant is that he was diligent even though he wasn't given as much as the first. He didn't say, "I didn't get the raise I deserved, the recognition I should, the boss doesn't give me the attention she gives others, so I'll coast." His attitude was, "I'm going to focus on the gracious opportunity entrusted to me." The second servant's response is important because if there are only two servants, you could conclude that effort should be based on what you receive. This guy proves that wrong!

We might call the third servant the Lazy Servant. Rather than doing something with what he was given, he puts it in the ground. On top of his laziness, he makes excuses. He's the person described in the book of Proverbs:

The sluggard says, "There is a lion in the road! There is a lion in the streets!" As a door turns on its hinges, so does a sluggard on his bed. The sluggard buries his hand in the dish; it wears him out to bring it back to his mouth. The sluggard is wiser in his own eyes than seven men who can answer sensibly. (Proverbs 26:13-16)

> *"We ask to know the will of God without guessing that his will is written into our very beings. We perceive that will when we discern our gifts."*
> — *Elizabeth O'Conner*

The real issue is this man refuses to take responsibility for his own lack of effort and in doing so is questioning the one who was gracious to him in the first place.

Our purpose and God's gifts go together. We are not given gifts to bury them but to use them, and by so doing we "enter the joy" of our Master. In other words, your purpose is more than a "job"; it's taking what God has given you and being diligent with it!

The **strengths** God has given you, be they a sharp mind, organizational skills, speaking ability, facility with numbers, being good with people, etc., are entrusted to you.

The **responsibilities** God has given you, your role in your family, work, and church, are entrusted to you, though they may change over time.

The **resources** God has given you, such as money, influence, or extra time, have been entrusted to you.

The Evaluation of the Master

Go back to the parable and notice the two evaluations the master gives. First, to those who had been hard at work, diligent in their efforts, and put their talent to work, the master says, "Well done, my good and faithful servant." To the third servant, the one who was slothful, the master says, "Cast him into darkness."

Seems a little harsh, doesn't it?

What elicited such different evaluations? The Diligent Servants were transformed by the gracious gift of the master. They went out with purpose, invested in the things of their master. The Lazy Servant deep down wasn't really all that interested in the master. He knew what to do but never did it. He blamed the master and made excuses for his laziness.

Are you motivated in this life to be diligent with what God has given you in order to advance His purposes? If not, this text demands the question, are you a Christian at all? Jesus says a disciple who is not motivated to work with diligence for His purposes in the world is no disciple at all.

God has entrusted each of us with specific abilities, responsibilities, and resources and has done so with purpose. We must be diligent in both discovering that purpose and fulfilling that purpose in order to be found faithful when the Master returns. The sooner we discover that purpose, the sooner we will become diligent in stewarding His gifts for His glory. Let us not be like those people in the subway that day, people surrounded by great opportunity, resources, and gifts and just walking right by.

Gifts Come in All Size Packages

Large Gifts

In 1 Corinthians 12:8-10, Paul gives examples of several spiritual gifts: words of wisdom, the word of knowledge, increased faith, the gifts of healing, the gift of miracles, prophecy, the discernment of spirits, diverse kinds of tongues, and interpretation of tongues. Later he also mentions the gifts of helping and the gifts of administration.

Gifting has both a nature and nurture component. You might naturally possess the spiritual gift of wisdom as a gift from the Lord. You grasp and learn things quickly. Your effort and experiences nurture that gift, perhaps driving you to love to study and experience things. It's important that you recognize this interaction and use it in your career and life.

Some may have an idea of their spiritual gift, but not know what to do with it or feel unclear on how to apply it in their lives. That's okay. The Dream and Achieve process will help you to not only discover your large-size gifts/elements but to drill down to get more specificity into what they are in order to give you a clearer path on how to apply them into your life/career.

Medium Gifts

Having a life-long partner is truly a gift from above. Someone to have and to hold, a partner with mutual trust, is an amazing gift. The Bible says that children and grandchildren are also gifts from the Lord (for example, Psalm 127:3). Friendship, health, and finances are other important gifts.

Your experiences are a gift: multiple years spent in the healthcare industry, 10+ years with the same company, a variety of exposures to different business experiences like turnaround, merger and acquisition, grass roots start-up experience, etc.

Our experiences (Lance's and Wes's) brought us to where we are today, teaching Tend Your Garden:

> *Lance*: The reason I can do what I do now as an executive coach is through my acquired professional experience across seven different countries, different business scopes, and in various job levels from sales representative to president.

> *Wes*: The reason I can do what I do now as founder of Lead Well Ministries, Inc., is that through my 23 years of ministry I've been in the local church, taught in seminaries, trained people in a global context, and been a part of different things from leading a megachurch to leading a mission team. All of these experiences are God's gifts in my life.

Small Gifts

Gifts in small-size packages may seem insignificant, but they are in fact important.

The sheer joy of doing something from a hobby to an activity to an experience is significant. If, for example, you love writing, why not have it as a key part of your career?

Isn't this Paul's point when he argues that the hand cannot say to the foot "I do not need you"? In God's economy, what we see as insignificant God uses for significant purposes. In the same way that Paul would say there is no insignificant gift within the church (hands, feet, etc.), we believe that there is no insignificant gift within your life. He has given all your gifts on purpose for purpose, both great and small.

Everyone Has Many Gifts

When you consider your large, medium, and small gifts, you'll see you actually have many gifts. Therefore, it's critical you have all of them in your life in some combination. You may not have all of them to a great degree, but you also cannot ignore any of them. Having a great career at the expense of your health, for instance, is a bad combination, or rather, neglecting the combination altogether. You need some level of balance.

Balance is like a good, healthy diet. You've seen the food pyramid. It shows how it is important to have all the food groups represented in your diet in some combination to maintain a healthy life.

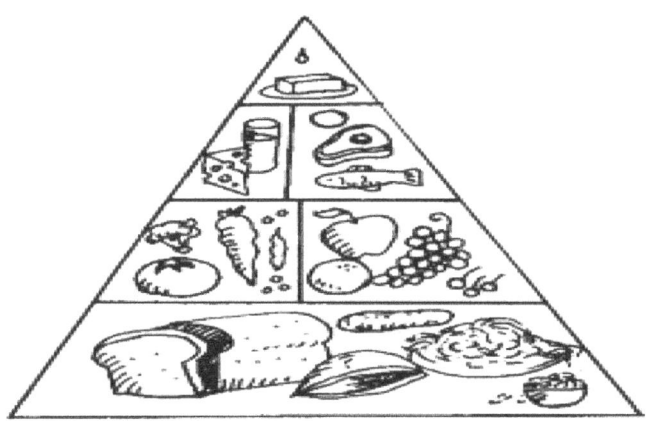

The Food Pyramid

If you ignore fruit for example, you're more prone to digestive ailments. If you don't eat any fish (Omega 3's and 6's), you may increase your risk of cardiovascular disease, cancer, or inflammatory diseases.

Like a healthy diet, your garden is made up of your many gifts that you need in some-kind-of-balance in your professional and personal life, and in your secular and Christian life.

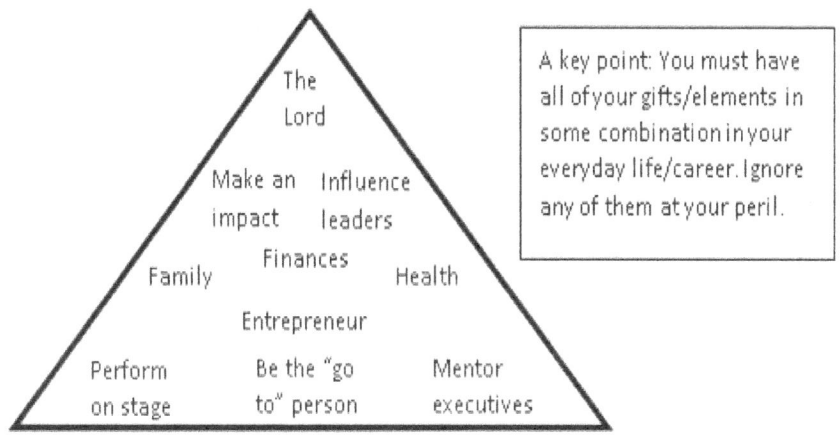

Inside triangle:
The Lord
Make an impact   Influence leaders
Family   Finances   Health
Entrepreneur
Perform on stage   Be the "go to" person   Mentor executives

Box: A key point: You must have all of your gifts/elements in some combination in your everyday life/career. Ignore any of them at your peril.

Wes's Story

This is a good place to share my (Wes's story), because it is about changing course in order to use many of my gifts.

Nudge

I spent 23 years in local church ministry. I had served in many areas: missions, adult discipleship, student ministry, and for over a decade as a lead pastor. I taught at three different seminaries. I was by all measures experiencing enormous success. I was leading one of the top 10 fasting growing churches in America, taking a single-campus church to three different campuses in a few short years, and I had published my first book. Yet, for several months, I found myself struggling to find peace vocationally. I felt like I wanted to make a bigger impact for the kingdom.

Then, out-of-nowhere, came a life crisis. After several conversations and seeking godly wisdom, I began to see this as God's nudging me in the direction I'd been struggling with for many months.

Discovery

It was time for a new direction, namely to step out in faith and take all the leadership lessons, teaching, speaking, training, writing, etc., from 23 years of ministry as the gifts from God they were. It was time to start my own ministry. It was not that I wanted to stop doing local church ministry, but it was clear that God was taking me in a new direction. I saw that the many different things I was doing, as successful as I was, spread me too thin. My own ministry would allow me to bring together my many gifts into a coherent role. It was a direction I may never been willing to go had that unfortunate crisis never happened.

Action

As a result, I started Lead Well Ministries, Inc. This ministry covers lots of areas that God has given me experience, gifting, and passions for. From leadership development and coaching, to teaching and preaching the Bible, to training pastors internationally, and writing, God has refocused His gifting in my life for a bigger kingdom impact.

Living God's Plan

God is still revealing His plan for both my life and for Lead Well Ministries, Inc. I am trusting God to open new and exciting doors where he can leverage my strengths and God-given passions to teach, train, and transform lives. While I am grateful for the many years of seeking to impact a local church for the sake of the gospel, there is an excitement and freedom to impact a larger community. God has taken my garden and expanded it for my enjoyment and His glory.

Don't Look for the "Answer"

Instructions from Scripture: Stop Waiting for the Answer

> Walter Houston, described by family members as a devoted Christian, died [one] Monday after waiting 70 years for God to give him clear direction about what to do with his life.
>
> "He hung around the house and prayed a lot, but just never got that confirmation," his wife Ruby said. "Sometimes he thought he heard God's voice, but then he wouldn't be sure, and he'd start the process all over again."
>
> Houston, she says, never really figured out what his life was about, but felt content to pray continuously about what he might do for the Lord. Whenever he was about to take action, he would pull back "because he didn't want to disappoint God or go against him in any way," Ruby says. "He was very sensitive to always remain in God's will. That was primary to him."
>
> Friends say they liked Walter though he seemed not to capitalize on his talents. "Walter had a number of skills he never got around to using," says longtime friend Timothy Burns. "He worked very well with wood and had a storyteller side to him, too. I always told him, 'Take a risk. Try something new if you're not happy,' but he was too afraid of letting the Lord down."

The above story isn't real, but it sure could be. It was an article published several years ago by Lark News, a Christian comedy/parody website. But even though the story is not real, the joke is based on a reality for many people. Far too often, people of faith use the excuse of "waiting on the will of God" to justify their lack of action. They treat the will of God as some mystical, secret plan that is extremely complicated to understand. As a result, they hesitate to take direct action or to step out in faith.

This happens in a lot of areas. Some people may avoid getting married because they are looking for the perfect companion. Others may avoid getting a job because they are waiting on the perfect situation. If we are not careful, we can find ourselves justifying our own fear, anxiety, confusion, or outright laziness on spiritual grounds—like Walter Houston.

Many do this out of sincerity of heart, that is, they aren't trying to be disobedient. They sincerely want to please God. But the real question concerns our beliefs about the will of God: *Is the will of God something you must know before you act, or is it something you will discover as you act?*

What does the Bible say about the will of God? Scripture speaks of the will of God in three main ways:

A Will of Decree: The Things God Has Determined Will Come to Pass

If the Scripture is clear on one thing it is this: God is sovereign over what happens in the world. Consider some passages:

> In him we have obtained an inheritance, having been predestined according to the purpose of him who works all things according to the counsel of his will. (Ephesians 1:11)

> Are not two sparrows sold for a penny? And not one of them will fall to the ground apart from your Father. But even the hairs of your head are all numbered. (Matthew 10:29–30)

> Your eyes saw my unformed substance; in your book were written, every one of them, the days that were formed for me, when as yet there was none of them. (Psalms 139:16)

He works *all* things according to His will … a sparrow doesn't fall apart from the Father's knowledge … all our days are written—every one of them!

Now, this does not mean we, as humans, can fully understand *why* certain things happen, but there is no denying that God has a sovereign will over the things that come to pass. If God were not sovereign, He would not be God. Our response ought not be to play the role of the Divine and figure it all out, but to trust Him and submit our lives to Him.

There is nothing we can do to change the decreed will of God. His purposes will come to pass.

A Will of Design: The Things God Has Commanded Us To Do

Secondly, the Bible speaks of God's will in terms of specific things God wants from your life. These things usually come across as commands in Scripture. God wants you (i.e., it is His will) to be holy, honest, generous, and loving. As a person of faith, you don't have to sit around and ask yourself, "Is it God's will for me to punch this man in the face or to forgive him for insulting me?" We know from Scripture that God's design is forgiveness, not revenge.

That's God's design, that's God's will for you in that situation. And there are lots of black-and-white commands of God that help us know his design, direction, and will for our lives. But that still doesn't solve all the gray areas. Whom should I marry? What job should I take? What college does God want me to go to? That leads us to God's will of desire.

A Will of Desire: The Things God Desires for Us

Do not love the world or the things in the world. If anyone loves the world, the love of the Father is not in him. For all that is in the world—the desires of the flesh and the desires of the eyes and pride of life—is not from the Father but is from the world. And the world is passing away along with its desires, but whoever does the will of God abides forever. (1 John 2:15–17)

"The secret things belong to the Lord our God, but the things that are revealed belong to us and to our children forever, that we may do all the words of this law. (Deuteronomy 29:29)

There are "gray areas of life," the things we don't always know or understand. There are the things the world desires and the things God desires. Which are we to do? There are things that are "secret," that is, not obvious or clear at the time. Does God desire for me to marry her, take this job, move to this city? The decisions are not so much about "right or wrong" but "right or left," namely what direction in life does God want me to go?

When it comes to these areas, we find God's will not through waiting but by *acting*. We discover God's will by stepping out in faith and taking steps forward, and in that process, we discover His will. These things are not known in advance (or at least not usually), and the longer we remain passive the more disobedient we are to His will. We're not suggesting you don't ask for wisdom or pray before acting. Of course you do those things. But we are saying you won't actually know until you do something. Or let's put it this way: While it is always wise to think before you act, make sure you act after you think!

Stop Looking for True North (the "Answer")

This concept is sometimes described in nonspiritual terms as the idea of seeking your "True North." Your True North is often spoken of as if there is only one path, one occupation per person, and you will only find true satisfaction when you discover it. But this approach to life is a recipe for disaster. As we've just seen, Scripture shows us that there are some things out of our control and other things beyond our ability to know.

Don't look for the answer,
look for the direction.

Waiting for the definitive answer or to find True North before taking action is simply the secular version of Walter Houston Syndrome. For most, it ends up in no progress at all.

That's why we say: When it comes to finding purpose in your life, don't look for the answer, look for the direction.

Marie Forleo, in her book *Everything is Figureoutable*, has this to say about taking action: "We think we need to achieve clarity before we can act, but the reality is the other way around: we gain clarity by acting."

I met a man who was looking most of his life for the answer, his mission, why God put him on this earth—his True North. He was an accounting manager for a consumer goods company. Having a passion for discipling men, he longed for a job that would leverage his experiences and allow him to disciple future leaders. He was waiting for the Lord to give him a distinct sign as to this role and where he should do it.

Because he was waiting for the answer and couldn't identify it himself, he didn't take any action. He stayed in his accounting manager role and thus got no closer to his dream. This is a common occurrence with people who long to understand their mission.

Where does "no progress" get you? It keeps you in the same tired job, working for the same uninspiring boss, in an unhealthy state, missing important relationships, with an out-of-balance work-life combination, itching to achieve God's plan for you.

True North

Identifying the answer (True North) seems so precise and definitive. There's north, and there's a straight line to the destination.

But there are major issues with this model:

- It is hard to figure out. Most cannot.

- If you don't achieve it, you feel like you're a failure.

- Too much depends upon it. What happens if you work long and hard to get to True North, sacrificing things and people who are precious to you, only to find out it's not what you thought it would be? That's a depressing and discouraging thought.

- It's a static concept. When you get there, you're there. Then what? You may be happy for a moment, but then you will start looking for the next thing. Look at how the "preacher" of Ecclesiastes sets out to find the ultimate purpose in life and ends up calling it all "vanity." What is worse than never getting that "one thing" is getting that "one thing" and realizing it does not offer what it promised.

- It is limiting. There is only one option, leaving us little room for variety. Identifying you want to be the CEO of Alibaba is great. However, it's a low probability that Jack Ma will call you up to take over his job. Where does that leave you? With no other options. And I'm sure you would like to have a variety of options.

- It is unreasonably precise. True North is an exact direction pointing to Santa's house in the North Pole. One degree west or three degrees east is no longer true north. We tend to look for that perfect something. Let's say you think, "There is only one person that can make me happy in marriage." What happens if you find her, but she marries someone else? Does that mean you'll never be happy? The idea of "only one" is too precise; it is bad math. Better to believer there are "types" of people that suit you best, or people who share certain things with you such as your faith, convictions, physical attraction, etc.

North, on the other hand—just *plain north*—is much broader and has room for your many gifts (strengths and passions). Therefore, we believe it is a better concept. This diagram shows the expansiveness of north, comprised of your many gifts versus the one point of True North:

North

Make an impact   Be the "go to" person   Perform on stage   Influence leaders

Family   The Lord   Health

Finances   Entrepreneur

North   Mentor executives   North

- It's much easier to figure out.

- As you take steps in a northerly direction, you gain more clarity on your purpose.

- As you take steps, you can make course corrections and still be on course.

- It doesn't require radical steps.

North is much broader and provides a variety of options and balance. A shift 20° west or 15° east still has you heading north. More options are always better. North opens up all of God's gifts for you to enjoy, use, and multiply.

Transformation Story: Jane Chao Finds Her North

Jane is the Co-founder and CEO of Ceribell Inc. When I first met Jane in 2011, she was an Engagement Manager for a Big 3 consulting firm in China. She was proud of her accomplishment of getting into this prestigious organization, but she knew there was more. She intuitively realized (the nudge) that there were important things missing in her life and career from finding her life partner to using her love of chemistry/biology to having an impact on society. Going through the DNA® process in a few short months, Jane discovered her garden, her North. This was the beginning of her process of taking a series of steps that ultimately lead to her co-founding the medical device company, Ceribell Inc.

A diagram of Jane's North would look like this:

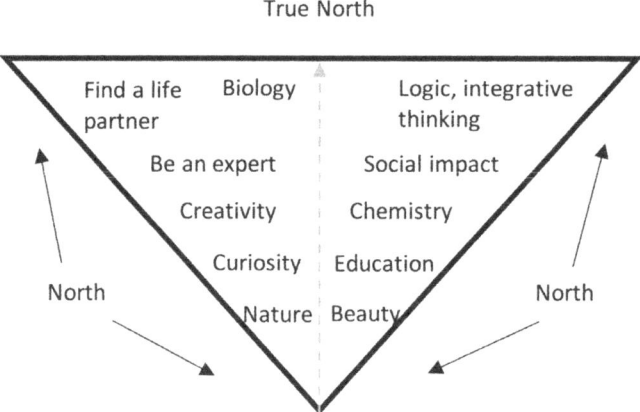

Still not sure you know how to find your North? Don't worry; we're about to turn to that next. The Dream and Achieve, or DNA, tool will help you identify your north and take steps to start moving toward it.

PART TWO:

Using the Dream and Achieve (DNA) Method to Plant Your Seeds

STEP 1 – Identify Your DNA® ELEMENTS

Identify Your Passions

Instructions from Scripture: Passion is Powerful

Bill Bowerman was the track and field coach at the University of Oregon between 1949 and 1972 and was also responsible for jump-starting the running and fitness movement that's popular today. If you are not familiar with his name, you are familiar with the company he co-founded a company named Nike.

Several years ago, there was a *Sport's Illustrated* article about Bowerman's life from one of his former runners, Kenny Moore. Moore described Bowerman as the kind of coach that would not let his players settle for mediocrity. He was always challenging them, never letting them settle for second best: "I was 20 years old," he writes, "had never won a race in high school, had never broken a 9:15 for two miles and one wet day in May [Bowerman] looked at me and said, 'Are you just in this to do mindless labor?'"

Moore adds that his coach inspired him not only in words and speeches but in the way he approached every single day: "He seemed to awaken each morning with new eyes."

We learn from Moore's story that Bowerman's impact on his players flowed from his passion for what he did—and that passion inspired those around him.

Someone once said that "the most untutored person with passion is more persuasive than the most eloquent without."

There are many examples of this in Scripture, but one of the clearest ones is from a man named Nehemiah:

> In the month of Nisan, in the twentieth year of King Artaxerxes, when wine was before him, I took up the wine and gave it to the king. Now, I had not been sad in his presence. And the king said to me, "Why is your face sad, seeing you are not sick? This is nothing but sadness of the heart."
>
> Then I was very much afraid. I said to the king, "Let the king live forever! Why should not my face be sad, when the city, the place of my fathers' graves, lies in ruins, and its gates have been destroyed by fire?"
>
> Then the king said to me, "What are you requesting?" So I prayed to the God of heaven. And I said to the king, "If it pleases the king, and if your servant has found favor in your sight, that you send me to Judah, to the city of my fathers' graves, that I may rebuild it."
>
> And the king said to me (the queen sitting beside him), "How long will you be gone, and when will you return?" So it pleased the king to send me when I had given him a time.
>
> And I said to the king, "If it pleases the king, let letters be given me to the governors of the province Beyond-the-River (Trans-Euphrates), that they may let me pass through until I come to Judah, and a letter to Asaph, the keeper of the king's forest, that he may give me timber to make beams for the gates of the fortress of the temple, and for the wall of the city, and for the house that I shall occupy." And the king granted me what I asked, for the good hand of my God was upon me. (Nehemiah 2:2–8)

Nehemiah had a passion for the people of God and their worship of God. When the king interacted with him, it was obvious something was burdening him. While on the surface it may have come across as sadness, that sadness was born out of a deep conviction to see the temple wall rebuilt so that the people of God could resume their worship of God. In Nehemiah's poignant words, "Why should not my face be sad, when the city, the place of my fathers' graves, lies in ruins, and its gates have been destroyed by fire?"

Nehemiah had a burden, a conviction, a passion in his life, and it was obvious to everyone around him. It compelled him to take action; he could not accept the status quo any longer. There was something in the world that had to be different, and Nehemiah wanted to do everything he could to make sure something was done about it.

Let me ask you: What are you passionate about? When you look around the world, your organization, your community, your family, what do you wake up every morning with "new eyes" for? Take a moment to reflect below:

_____

_____

_____

_____

_____

The reason that is such an important question is because…

Great leaders have passion

Great leaders approach life with a sense of calling. They don't do what they do because they are forced to or merely to earn a paycheck but because they have a passion to do what they do. By passion, I don't mean a wild, reckless, overbearing personality—I mean a deeply held commitment or conviction that drives you in your life.

_____

"Above all else, guard your heart,
For everything you do flows from it."
—Proverbs 4:23

_____

Great leaders may not want to change the world, but they want to change something in the world. There is something about the status quo that he or she can no longer accept. Martin Luther King, Jr., a great leader if ever there was one, put it like this:

> If it falls to your lot to be a street sweeper, sweep the streets like Michelangelo painted pictures, like Shakespeare wrote poetry, like Beethoven composed music; sweep streets so well that all the host of Heaven and earth will have to pause and say, "Here lived a great street sweeper, who swept his job well."

Passion is such a key part of being a great leader that if you don't have it, you simply can't be a great leader.

Four Reasons Why Great Leaders Must Have Passion

Passion Inspires People

People will sacrifice, go the extra mile, when they really care about what they are doing. The "why" of your business has to be so big that it keeps you on fire and ignites your team.

Passion Produces Purpose

Howard Hendricks, a professor at Dallas Theological Seminary, taught his preachers-in-training that "Your career is what you're paid to do; your calling is what you're made to do." You need to know your passion, your conviction, the thing that breaks your heart because until you find out what that is, you'll settle for purposelessness. You find your purpose when you find your passion.

Eric Liddell was a famous Olympic runner; the movie *Chariots of Fire* was based off his life. He once said, "I believe God made me for a purpose, but he also made me fast. When I run I feel His pleasure." What do you feel you were made to do? What is it that, when you do that thing, it makes you feel like you are doing what God has called you to do?

Is it possible that there is a reason you're most passionate about that thing? That maybe the very purpose you've been given is directly related to the passion burning in your heart? Great leaders are great because they endow others with their passion and purpose.

Passion Fuels Perseverance

Leadership is hard. Leaders who truly inspire others towards a vision will face criticism and conflict. Therefore, if you don't have a deep conviction about what you are doing, it will be easy to pack it in and throw in the towel. Passion keeps you going even when times are difficult.

Passion Leaves a Path

Have you ever played dominoes? The first domino never actually makes contact with the last one, yet the action of the first makes an impact on the last. You need to think of your life in this way, namely, when you get intense and pour into someone else it has an impact on generations to come! But it all starts with one.

Many years from now, what would you like people to line up and thank you for? You have no idea what hangs in the balance of you taking action on the thing that burdens you the most for your company, family, and community.

What is it that makes you wake up each day with "new eyes"?

Your Passions Are Where You Have Energy

A McKinsey study on centered leadership showed that meaning (purpose and passion) is five times more powerful than any other dimension of leadership in affecting employees' general satisfaction. One key reason is that of all the energies needed to perform at your peak, spiritual energy (feeling purpose, living your passion, doing what you were meant to do) is the most self-renewing. If every day you could have a career that allowed you to use your strengths and passions, you would be productive and create amazing results. Continuing this day-after-day can bring you to distinctiveness.

The most critical leadership skill? According to James Kouzes and Barry Posner in their book *Learning Leadership*, it's the ability to learn. And you can learn to be a passionate leader!

They say you need to "Take initiative for your own leadership development" by first learning "who you are." Then you should not be asking yourself, "Will I make a difference?" but rather, "How will I make the difference I want?"

In other words, be an authentic leader by forging and living out the vision you want to create.

Identifying your passions using the DNA® Workbook

> To start your journey, we will use the Dream and Achieve Workbook. Open the workbook now and find the worksheet "Step 1 Elements" (look for the tab at the bottom left of the screen). Follow the instructions to complete the **Passions** column. (Note: Ignore the Coach Code column for now.)

To identify your passions, ask some open-ended questions. What do I love to do? What would I enjoy doing every day? What job would I enjoy doing even though I may not get paid? What motivates me? What is important to me? What do I value most in my life? What do I feel is missing?

Here's how we filled out our Passions columns:

Lance Tanaka DNA Transformation: Passions

Be the "go to" person
Be healthy naturally: look good, feel good, look & feel young
Be a great role model to my two children, Matthew and Michael
Strong marriage with my wife, Renee
Work with people I enjoy
Be a mentor to business executives, young professionals, university students
Have a great family
Influence the influential
Serve my Lord
Have a dream home in the U.S. and Asia
Get people to stop making excuses to take action
Play music weekly
Have a beer with the guys
Frequent public speaking
Fun debate, be a catalyst to interesting discussion
Being on stage
Live in Asia, frequent visits to U.S.
Be a part of history: China's rapid development
Have an impact
Playing sports: tennis, baseball
Be recognized and respected
Eating cheap food or expensive food
Having control and freedom
Feeling good, making progress, taking action
Financial freedom, security
Help people discover & leverage their gifting
My brother
Close circle of friends
Freedom

Wes Feltner Transformation: Passions

Preaching and teaching
Training leaders
Travel
Fitness and staying healthy
Being intentional with my three children
Enjoying a cigar and listening to music
Reading and learning
Financial freedom and living debt free
Fishing
Watching Kentucky basketball
Providing for my family
Starting a business or speaking platform outside of a local church
Teaching at seminaries
Laughter and making others laugh
Enjoying finer things in life/Quality as important as quantity
Mission trips and helping others in need

If your list isn't as long as ours, yet, don't worry. We want you to take 15 minutes each day for the next 20 days to add more items to your list. That may feel like a lot, but you will find that this repetitive process unlocks your unconscious mind. It's important for you to make this little investment in yourself. It may be one of the most important exercises of the brain and heart you will ever take.

Identify Your Strengths

It's one of the most disappointing sports stories of the last decade. If you follow football even casually, you've likely heard the name Johnny Manziel (a.k.a., Johnny Football). Johnny played college football for Texas A&M and had a very successful college career: he broke numerous records (only freshman to pass for 3,000 yards and rush for 1,000) and won numerous awards (David O'Brien award for top QB, first team all-American, all SEC, and even won the Heisman trophy). He was amazing to watch on the field.

That's why, in 2014, the Cleveland Browns selected him in the first round of the NFL draft. Manziel's future looked bright and expectations were high. But his life quickly spiraled out of control. A life of partying, casinos, in-and-out of alcohol treatment centers, and allegations of domestic violence soon caused his NFL career to end as quickly as it started. His agent left him, his sponsor Nike dropped him, and the Cleveland Browns eventually cut him.

Several months later, Johnny Manziel informed the sports world he planned to make a comeback. Whether or not much of a comeback ever occurred, what Manziel said was still very interesting: "I refuse to let my entire life of sports from the age of four be squandered by partying." In other words, Johnny got to the point where he was tired of wasting his life, tired of wasting all the talents and gifts he'd been given.

Most of us can relate to that frustration, namely the feeling of looking back on something and feeling like it was wasted or squandered, feeling like we wasted time (*What did I accomplish?*), relationships (*I gave her two years of my life and for what?*), money (*This is a piece of junk!*), opportunities (*I wish I could go back and do that over again.*), or worst of all, a wasted life (*Did my life count for anything important?*). When it comes to gifts, talents, and opportunities, we're talking about things that are not meant to be wasted but leveraged with intentionality and purpose.

Instructions from Scripture: You Have a Gift, Use It

Notice what the Apostle Peter says as it relates to our gifts:

> The end of all things is at hand; therefore be self-controlled and sober-minded for the sake of your prayers. Above all, keep loving one another earnestly, since love covers a multitude of sins. Show hospitality to one another without grumbling. As each has received a gift, use it to serve one another, as good stewards of God's varied grace: whoever speaks, as one who speaks oracles of God; whoever serves, as one who serves by the strength that God supplies—in order that in everything God may be glorified through Jesus Christ. To him belong glory and dominion forever and ever. Amen. (1 Peter 4:7–11)

Peter does not want his readers to be "Johnny Manziel"-type believers, the kind of believers who have all these gifts yet never use them or leverage them for their good and God's glory.

To leverage your gifts purposefully, you have to wake up! Peter says, "be focused" and "alert" so that you don't waste your opportunity. When you stop and think about the time you have in this life and in this world, it's really not a lot. Life is like a vapor. One day the kids are born and the next day they are off to college. One day you are starting the job and the next day they are throwing your retirement party. Therefore, Peter says, get after it, get going, get focused, don't waste what you've been given. Use it!

Peter here is only repeating what Jesus taught him and the disciples in Luke 12:

> Stay dressed for action and keep your lamps burning and be like men who are waiting for their master to come home from the wedding feast, so that they may open the door to him at once when he comes and knocks. Blessed are those servants whom the master finds awake when he comes. Truly, I say to you, he will dress himself for service and have them recline

at table and he will come and serve them. If he comes in the second watch, or in the third, and finds them awake, blessed are those servants… You also must be ready, for the Son of Man is coming at an hour you do not expect. (Luke 12:35–38, 40)

The New Testament never invites believers to withdraw from the world and gaze at the skies because the end is near. The imminence of the end should function as a stimulus to action in this world. The knowledge that believers are sojourners and exiles, whose time is short, should galvanize them to make their lives count now. If not now, when? You aren't getting younger and His return is getting closer!

Peter says, "You have a gift, use it." If speaking, speak. If serving, serve. Every Christian has a gift that they are called to use for others. And the reason why this is so important is when you do not use God's gifts you become useless to God's purposes!

Take, for instance, the Dead Sea. It is 50 miles long and 11 miles wide and yet completely dead and useless for life. Why? It has no outlet. Minerals flow from the Sea of Galilee into the Jordan River and then into the Dead Sea, but nothing ever leaves. There's no turning over, no renewal. What makes the Dead Sea dead is that it is always receiving and never doing.

Life is full of examples, like Johnny Manziel, of people who have wasted their life. They are physical examples of what the Bible warns us about spiritually. So, think about the time you have, talent you've been given, or opportunities that are before you. Why? Because while I have no idea if Johnny Manziel will ever come back, I am certain Jesus will. And because we believe that day could be any day, let's not squander our gifts but leverage them for the good of others and the glory of God.

We Thrive When We Play to Our Strengths

Be more of who you were designed by God to be. To become distinctive, you need to leverage your strengths into towering strengths. Therefore, identify them, develop plans to further develop them, and get more of them into your career and life. And the Lord will bless you as you use them.

Your Brain is Hard-Wired for Your Strengths and Weaknesses

A Gallup study of 2,000 businesses measured on productivity, profitability, and employee retention found that managers who used a strengths-based approach with their reports are twice as likely to be high performing as other managers.

When I [Lance] was a child, I was poor in math. My parents did what most Asian parents would do: They got me a math tutor. Every night with my tutor I went through hell. After three months of working hard, night after night, I was able to take my math skills from poor up to … slightly better than poor.

Think about it: Like many other people's weaknesses, my poor math skills are hard-wired into my brain. And we all know how difficult it is to rewire the brain. Focusing on fixing your weaknesses will at best make you average. There is nothing wrong with average. If you want to be average, this is a good approach.

However, many of us want to be exceptional at something. If you want to be distinctive, you need to identify your strengths and leverage them by focusing on developing them even further. Choose classes in them, enroll in training courses that will enhance them, and get involved in projects that will help you further advance them. Because your brain is hard-wired for your strengths, it takes less effort to dramatically improve them.

The Lord wants your best. Focusing on and further developing your strengths, that is, the gifts He gave you, can deliver excellence.

Identifying Your Strengths using the DNA® Workbook

To identify your strengths, ask yourself: What do I do well? What seems to take little effort in doing a good job? What do people admire about me? What are my talents?

> *To continue your journey, go to the Dream and Achieve Workbook, Step 1: Elements worksheet and follow the instructions to fill out the Strengths column.*

Be as specific as possible. Writing down that you are "good with people" is too general. Are you good at meeting people for the first time? Are you good at reading their feelings and emotions? Are you good at making friends quickly? Are you good at influencing them? Are you good at developing strong, loyal, relationships?

Don't judge what you write down. Turn yourself loose and write down whatever comes to mind. Ask friends, family, and anyone who knows you well what they think are your strengths. Pray and ask the Lord for wisdom.

Here are our Strengths columns:

Wes Feltner Transformation: Strengths

Leadership and Casting Vision
Preaching and Teaching
Public speaking
Making complex concepts easy to understand
Strong Drive and work ethic
Very focused and willing to say "No" to lesser things
Athletic and active
Ability to relate with others
Team-building
Financially disciplined
Inspirational
20+ years of preaching

Lance Tanaka Transformation: Strengths

Motivate people to take action
Read people: are they telling the truth, are they interested, do they believe me?
Generalist: can do many things average or above, but an expert at nothing
Music: especially in evoking emotion
Goal/target achievement
Daily discipline to get things done
Public speaking: motivating people
Pick up new skills quite easily
People open up to me quickly, tell me their problems and stories
Hard worker
Pick up new skills quite easily
Cross-culture understanding Asia-West
Highly organized
Influence people
Getting things done, taking action
Executive experience in Fortune 500 companies

As with the Passions list, add to this list 15 minutes each day for 20 days.

Transformation Story: Darren Ho's Transformation from Marketer to Leader

Nudge

Darren always had leadership roles from high school to college and in his business career, but his transformation began as a series of nudges.

Nudge #1 was the realization he could influence people from asking questions. In 2007, he was in the Six Sigma leadership development program. The primary focus of this tool was to ask questions and solve problems, which played to a strength and fed his passion to influence others.

His company sent him and his family to China from 2009–2014, where he took a marketing leadership role and became a Six Sigma Champion. This experience stoked the fire in him to leverage and build his skills around asking questions, leading him to look into executive coaching to further expand the company's people management skills.

Coaching was very much aligned to his passion, and it led to Nudge #2. He felt driven to help people understand themselves on a more holistic approach than could be accomplished via the insular metrics of a corporation.

Discovery

Like most of us, Darren was first doing things for his own glory, his career. However, after accepting Jesus as his savior, his attitude evolved until he was doing everything for His glory and seeking to use his company platform to reach more people.

Through the DNA® process, Darren discovered the key elements that made up his North. These included the need to have willing participants who want to grow and the desire to impact the whole of people's lives, co-creating life plans between coach and coachee.

Action

After discovering coaching was his future vocation, Darren got certified in coaching, completing a three-year process in just one (that's called passion!). He also sought out mentors, including Lance, a Master Coach, who mentored and certified him in the DNA® tool. He did further research on whole-life disciple making. To further integrate his secular and Christian life, Darren went to seminary in 2010 to grow his theological understanding.

Living God's Plan

This process helped him to evolve toward a completely different career, from a marketing, Six Sigma champion to an executive coach who helps people grow holistically. He learned to leverage his company's platform to further build his coaching skills, further ignite his passion to developing people, and create and expand the company's leadership/coaching development programs in China and the world.

STEP 2 - DNA® DRILL DOWN

Find Your Elements

The statement I (Wes) am about to make will reveal how old I'm getting: I remember the days of Blockbuster Video. There, I said it. Now, for those who have no idea what I'm talking about, back in Old Testament times if you wanted to rent a movie you had to get on your camel (the Ancient Near Eastern version of Uber), go to *an actual store*, pick up an *actual video* from a shelf. Sometimes, (wait for it…) it wasn't in stock. This meant you couldn't watch it that night! [It was a dry and weary land where there was no iTunes].

But for those of us who remember these ancient days of 2004, Blockbuster was the big name in entertainment. Then a company came along that offered the same entertainment experience from the comfort of your home. You didn't have to drive to the store and hope they had the video you wanted. They would mail you the DVD, you could keep it as long as you wanted (no late fees), and then you could mail it back when you were finished.

Before long, they started offering online streaming. By now you know I'm speaking of the company Netflix. At the end of 2019, Netflix was a $60 billion company with 140 million subscribers; Blockbuster, on the other hand, is gone (except for, like, one store in Alaska or something).

What happened? Around 2006/07, Netflix was struggling and approached Blockbuster to buy them out, but Blockbuster refused. Within 18 months, Blockbuster lost 85% of its value and within two years was bankrupt. Why? Blockbuster lost focus on their purpose. They become so consumed in the "one thing" they were doing, they didn't consider the other options that were specifically related to their purpose. You see, Blockbuster was not in the video business, they were in the entertainment business, and their "single focus" mindset caused them to drift away into the fog of irrelevance.

This is really easy to do in life. We become so consumed with work, we lose focus on our families. We become so consumed with money, we lose focus on relationships. And the danger is we drift into purposelessness.

Instructions from Scripture: There are Multiple Elements (Gifts) in Your Garden

When it comes to tending your garden, you need to realize it isn't just one thing, it is actually multiple things. Let's go back to the garden in Genesis again.

Was the only purpose for the garden vocational work, i.e., tending the ground? Of course not! There were other things that came along with tending his garden that had everything to do with obedience to his God-given purpose.

For example, in addition to cultivating the ground, Adam was to cultivate a marriage ("a man shall leave his father and mother and be joined to his wife"). In addition to cultivating a marriage, Adam and Eve were to cultivate children ("be fruitful and multiple"). They were given stewardship over animals and many other things ("let them have dominion over the birds of the air," etc.). *There were multiple elements within the single garden!*

One of the most important things in tending your garden is finding the balance between the things that matter, the things God has placed within your garden. Think of your garden as having different things to care for.

So just like in an actual garden there may be several different rows of different types of vegetables, they are still all a part of the same garden. A good and faithful gardener must not neglect any of the crops within the garden. Balance is required for obedience. In the same way, we must not become like Blockbuster, so single-focused on one thing, that we neglect the other parts of what we've been called to steward.

How to Find Your Elements

Let's clarify your journey. Go to the Dream and Achieve Workbook, Step 1: Elements worksheet.

Now that you've completed your Strengths and Passions lists in Step 1, you need to analyze the lists to find common "elements." Elements are the cross-roads between your strengths, experiences, and passions. These are the very things you need to have in your career and life to be successful and fulfilled. We find that most people need between 7–10 elements.

Here are the elements we discovered through this exercise:

Lance Tanaka Transformation: Elements

- Highly influential: be the "go to" impact person

- Develop, mentor, and influence

- Performing on stage

- Help people discover and leverage their gifting

- Finance: Have freedom with financial security

- Most important relationships: The Lord; wife, Renee; two sons, Matt and Michael

- Fitness/health: Maintain weight; don't gain beyond 1 lb., look good naturally

Wes Feltner Transformation: Elements

- Preaching and teaching

- Starting a business or speaking platform outside of a local church

- Public speaking

- Finance: Live debt free, pay off house in 10 years or less

- Finance: College for kids

- Fitness/health: Fitness and staying healthy, eating clean, and feeling good

- Most important relationships: The Lord; wife, Stephanie; kids, Caleb, Audrey, Ashlyn

Your list of elements will also have *finance*, *fitness/health*, and *relationships* components in addition to your strengths and passions.

We have been blessed with many gifts from our Lord: loving family; relationships; health; finances; various strengths, passions, experiences; and above all grace. Therefore, it's critical for us to identify what they are and then use them and multiply them as the Diligent Servants multiplied their talents. In order for us to multiply our gifts, we need to take steps to leverage them. But we must first understand them more deeply: the who, what, where, and when for each of them.

On the Step 1 worksheet, you need to code your passions in column B and strengths in column E. Your coach will send you their code suggestions. You then need to make the necessary adjustments. For those of you without a coach, use the below procedure to code your lists.

Coding is the process of grouping each passion and strength into a broader category or umbrella. This needs to be done to identify common themes and consistencies between your strengths and passions. This will help you identify your elements/gifting/talents.

Take a look at how we coded our lists and then read on for instructions on how to code your own.

Lance Tanaka Transformation: Codes

I used codes like "Impact," "Infl" (influence), and "Rel" (relationships). It's clear to me that "impact" is a resonating code for me. As you can see, it shows up over and over in both lists.

Passions	Code	Strengths	Code
Be the "go to" person.	Impact	Motivate people to take action	Infl
Be healthy naturally: look good, feel good, look and feel young	Health	Read people: are they telling the truth, are they interested	Infl
Be a great role model to my two children, Matthew and Michael	Rel	Generalist: can do many things average or above, but an expert at nothing	
Strong marriage with my wife, Renee	Rel	Music: especially in evoking emotion	Perf
Work with people I enjoy	Peop	Goal/target achievement	Impact
Be a mentor to business execs, young professionals, univ students	Infl	Daily discipline to get things done	Impact
Have a great family	Rel	Public speaking: motivating people	Perf
Influence the influential	Infl	Pick up new skills quite easily	
Serve my Lord	Rel	People open up to me quickly, tell me their problems and stories	Infl
Have a dream home in the U.S. and Asia	Fin	Hard worker	Impact
Get people to stop making excuses to take action	Impact	Pick up new skills quite easily	

Play music weekly	Perf	Cross-culture understanding Asia-West	Infl
Have a beer with the guys	Rel	Highly organized	Impact
Frequent public speaking	Perf	Influence people	Infl
Fun debate, be a catalyst to interesting discussion	Impact	Getting things done, taking action	Impact
Being on stage	Perf	Executive experience in Fortune 500 companies	Impact
Live in Asia, frequent visits to U.S.	Geo		
Be a part of history: China's rapid development	Impact		
Have an impact	Impact		
Playing sports: tennis, baseball	Health		
Be recognized and respected	Impact		
Eating cheap food or expensive food			
Having control and freedom	Fin		
Feeling good, making progress, taking action	Impact		
Financial freedom, security	Fin		
Help people discover and leverage their gifting	Impact		
My brother	Rel		
Close circle of friends	Rel		
Freedom	Impact		

"Influence" is also resonating code for me. It shows up throughout both lists.

Passions	Code	Strengths	Code
Be the "go to" person.	Impact	Motivate people to take action	Infl
Be healthy naturally: look good, feel good, look and feel young	Health	Read people: are they telling the truth, are they interested	Infl
Be a great role model to my two children, Matthew and Michael	Rel	Generalist: can do many things average or above, but an expert at nothing	
Strong marriage with my wife, Renee	Rel	Music: especially in evoking emotion	Perf
Work with people I enjoy	Peop	Goal/target achievement	Impact
Be a mentor to business execs, young professionals, univ students	Infl	Daily discipline to get things done	Impact
Have a great family	Rel	Public speaking: motivating people	Perf
Influence the influential	Infl	Pick up new skills quite easily	
Serve my Lord	Rel	People open up to me quickly, tell me their problems and stories	Infl
Have a dream home in the U.S. and Asia	Fin	Hard worker	Impact
Get people to stop making excuses to take action	Impact	Pick up new skills quite easily	
Play music weekly	Perf	Cross-culture understanding Asia-West	Infl
Have a beer with the guys	Rel	Highly organized	Impact
Frequent public speaking	Perf	Influence people	Infl

In addition, it's pretty obvious performing ("Perf") on stage, whether it's musical or public speaking is a key need for me to be happy and fulfilled.

Passions	Code	Strengths	Code
Be the "go to" person.	Impact	Motivate people to take action	Infl
Be healthy naturally: look good, feel good, look and feel young	Health	Read people: are they telling the truth, are they interested	Infl
Be a great role model to my two children, Matthew and Michael	Rel	Generalist: can do many things average or above, but an expert at nothing	
Strong marriage with my wife	Rel	Music: especially in evoking emotion	Perf
Work with people I enjoy	Peop	Goal/target achievement	Impact
Be a mentor to business execs, young professionals, univ students	Infl	Daily discipline to get things done	Impact
Have a great family	Rel	Public speaking: motivating people	Perf
Influence the influential	Infl	Pick up new skills quite easily	
Serve my Lord	Rel	People open up to me quickly, tell me their problems and stories	Infl
Have a dream home in U.S./Asia	Fin	Hard worker	Impact
Get people to stop making excuses to take action	Impact	Pick up new skills quite easily	
Play music weekly	Perf	Cross-culture understanding	Infl
Have a beer with the guys	Rel	Highly organized	Impact
Frequent public speaking	Perf	Influence people	Infl
Fun debate, be a catalyst to interesting discussion	Impact	Getting things done, taking action	Impact
Being on stage	Perf	Executive experience in Fortune 500 companies	Impact

Although there is only one item, for me, **"Help people discover and leverage their gifting"** is heavily weighted, so I chose it as a key element.

Now it's time shift to the Dream and Achieve Workbook, Step 2: Drill Down worksheet.

For Step 2, I took my coding and choose to highlight four items in the Elements list and wrote them down in Step 2 Cells A8–16:

- Highly influential: be the "go to" impact person

- Develop, mentor and influence

- Performing on stage

- Help people discover & leverage their gifting

Go ahead and do the same for yourself. Then, drill down on the Who for each element, that is, "Who receives this gift?" Continuing Lance's example, his Who column looks like this:

Element	Who
Highly influential be the "go to" impact person	Work with people I enjoy and the influential
Develop, mentor and influence	Matt, Michael, bus. execs, young pros, students, disciples
Performing on stage	Professionals, church, public
Help people discover and leverage their gifting	Christian leaders and secular leaders

Drill down on What for each of the elements, that is, "What does using this gift look like?"

Element	What
Highly influential be the "go to" impact person	Establish a company
Develop, mentor and influence	Motivate people to take action, leverage that people open up to me
Performing on stage	Seminars, speeches, workshops, church lead worship
Help people discover and leverage their gifting	Set up a DNA foundation

Drill down on Where for each of the elements: "Where would you use this gift?"

Element	Where
Highly influential be the "go to" impact person	Greater China
Develop, mentor and influence	Home, companies, associations, public venues, media, church
Performing on stage	Companies, associations, public venues, media, churches
Help people discover and leverage their gifting	China and U.S.

Now, drill down on When for each element: "When or how often would you like to implement/integrate/achieve this?"

Element	When
Highly influential be the "go to" impact person	By 2001
Develop, mentor and influence	Daily
Performing on stage	Weekly
Help people discover and leverage their gifting	Next career

For just about everyone, finance, fitness/health, and relationship elements are critical. Fill out your worksheet for each of these common elements.

Finance

- I want to have freedom with financial security

- My financial goals and targets are:

  - Hit ___ net worth target to retire in 2001

  - Dream home in U.S. by 2014

Fitness/Health

Priority #1: Maintain weight: don't gain beyond 1 lb.

Priority #2: Look good naturally

Relationships

- Most important to me: The Lord; wife, Renee; sons, Matt and Michael

- Missing: Close circle of friends

- To repair: Sister

Many of us need to have more balance in our life. In C31 and E31, I listed two important things to improve my work life balance:

- Limit travel

- Work on my retirement/foundation

Wes, of course, went through the same process to discover his own elements.

Wes Feltner Transformation: Elements

Preaching and teaching is a key element for me.

Passions	Code	Strengths	Code
Preaching and teaching	Teach/PS	Leadership and casting vision	Teach
Training leaders	Teach	Preaching and teaching	Teach/ps
Travel	Relax	Public speaking	PS
Fitness and staying healthy	Fit	Making complex concepts easy to understand	Teach
Being intentional with my three children	Fam	Strong drive and work ethic	Entrepre
Enjoying a cigar and listening to music	Relax	Very focused and willing to say "No" to lesser things	Focus
Reading and learning	Learn	Athletic and active	Fit
Financial freedom and living debt free	Fin	Ability to relate with others	Infl
Fishing	Relax	Team-building	Team
Watching Kentucky basketball	Relax	Financially disciplined	Fin
Providing for my family	Fin	Inspirational	Teach/PS
Starting a business or speaking platform outside of a local church	Entrepre	20+ years of preaching	Teach/PS
Teaching at seminaries	Teach/PS		
Laughter and making others laugh	Infl		
Enjoying finer things in life/Quality as important as quantity			
Mission trips and helping others in need	Teach		

Some of my strengths and passions also point to public speaking (PS) or being on stage.

Passions	Code	Strengths	Code
Preaching and teaching	teach/PS	Leadership and casting vision	teach
Training leaders	teach	Preaching and teaching	teach/PS
Travel	relax	Public speaking	PS
Fitness and staying healthy	fit	Making complex concepts easy to understand	teach
Being intentional with my three children	fam	Strong drive and work ethic	entrepre
Enjoying a cigar and listening to music	relax	Very focused and willing to say "No" to lesser things	focus
Reading and learning	learn	Athletic and active	fit
Financial freedom and living debt free	fin	Ability to relate with others	infl
Fishing	relax	Team-building	team
Watching Kentucky basketball	relax	Financially disciplined	fin
Providing for my children	fin	Inspirational	teach/PS
Starting a business or speaking platform outside of a local church	entrepre	20+ years of preaching	teach/PS
Teaching at seminaries	teach/PS		
Laughter and making others laugh	infl		
Enjoying finer things in life/Quality as important as quantity			
Mission trips and helping others in need	teach		

Although I was the lead pastor for a mega-church, I can envision in my next career being an entrepreneur. That would be highly motivating and energizing. It would certainly leverage my gifts, and though there are only two "entrepreneur" items, they feel heavily weighted for me.

Passions	Code		Strengths	Code
Preaching and teaching	teach/PS		Leadership and casting vision	teach
Training leaders	teach		Preaching and teaching	teach/PS
Travel	relax		Public speaking	PS
Fitness and staying healthy	fit		Making complex concepts easy to understand	teach
Being intentional with my three children	fam		Strong drive and work ethic	entrepre
Enjoying a cigar and listening to music	relax		Very focused and willing to say "No" to lesser things	focus
Reading and learning	learn		Athletic and active	fit
Financial freedom and living debt free	fin		Ability to relate with others	infl
Fishing	relax		Team-building	team
Watching Kentucky basketball	relax		Financially disciplined	fin
Providing for my children	fin		Inspirational	teach/PS
Starting a business or speaking platform outside of a local church	entrepre		20+ years of preaching	teach/PS
Teaching at seminaries	teach/PS			
Laughter and making others laugh	infl			
Enjoying finer things in life/Quality as important as quantity				
Mission trips and helping others in need	teach			

Moving on to Step 2, I took my coding and chose three elements to list:

- Preaching and teaching
- Starting a business or speaking platform outside of a local church
- Public speaking

Finance goals and targets

- Live debt free and payoff house in 10 years or less
- College for the kids starting 2024

Fitness/health

- Priority #1: Fitness and staying healthy

- Priority #2: Eating clean and feeling good

Relationships

- Most important to me: The Lord; wife, Stephanie; kids, Caleb, Audrey, Ashlyn

- Missing: none

- To repair: past friendships that haven't been reconciled (names not disclosed)

- Work life balance.

- Travel more globally

- Actually use vacation time and go fishing with Caleb more

Code Your Passions and Strengths

Now it's your turn to code your passions and strengths lists. Go to the Step 1 worksheet and fill out the codes as your coach suggested or with your own codes.

A few guard rails to consider when coding.

- There are no set codes. You can use any words to describe your strengths and passions. For Lance's coding, we used such codes as "impact," "influence," and "perform." You may use such codes as "develop people," "outreach," "teaching children."

- You don't need to code everything.

- Use codes that resonate with you.

- You may designate multiple codes to a single passion or strength. In Wes's case, we used the preaching code and public speaking code on a number of strengths and passions. "Teaching at seminars" can have two codes: teaching and public speaking.

Look for patterns to emerge. Choose three or four elements to list on the Step 2 worksheet (Cells A8–16).

Once you have your elements, it's time to drill down on the Who, What, When, and Where for each one.

WHO

Identify whom you want to impact both in general and specific terms.

- Age: e.g. kids, young managers, elderly, etc.

- Gender: e.g., male or female

- Type: e.g., students, professionals, executives, parents, married, secular, Christian, etc.

- Specific names: e.g., My sons, Matt and Michael

WHAT

Identify specific activities or skills: e.g., Teaching Mandarin language to English speakers, influencing people to follow me, establish a foundation, run seminars, give speeches, etc.

WHERE

- General locations: e.g., City or country, urban, nature, water, coast, forest, mountains, etc.

- Actual locations: e.g., Seattle, specific church or business, RZIM, etc.

- Location type: e.g., primary schools, office, factory, etc.

- Actual location: e.g., Hong Kong University, my home, my office, my church, etc.

WHEN

- How often: e.g., once per week, Mon and Fri, evenings, etc.

- Timing: e.g,. December, summer, next fall, etc.

- Actual date: March 15, 2020, etc.

Now think about your finance, fitness/health, and relationship elements.

FINANCES

Write down *two* financial goals and their target dates.

FITNESS/HEALTH

Write down *two* fitness/health priorities.

RELATIONSHIPS

Write the names of *three specific people* who are most important to you. Write down a key relationship that is missing in your life. Then identify and write down a specific relationship (name) that needs to be repaired.

BALANCE

Many of us need to have more balance in our life. Write down two important things you need to do to improve your work life balance.

Transformation Story: Lei Zuo (LZ) Grows Beyond His Regional Leadership Role

Nudge

LZ felt a clear call to steward his gifts. He knew he had been blessed with gifts and that he had a responsibility to use and leverage them; he certainly didn't want to be like the Lazy Servant.

A good friend of his spent 10 years serving in China but had to leave his post due to unexpected circumstances. This was the nudge or wake-up call LZ needed. He realized that his own time of service could end at any moment, and he wanted to leave China and his team in a better place than where he found it.

Discovery

LZ joined us for the Dream and Achieve course. Working with LZ over a few sessions, we were able to clarify his elements:

- Extract potential
- Make an impact
- Growth not turnaround
- Industry: not a concern
- Product: not a concern
- China
- Your role in an organization: leader, go to, influencer, but don't have to be the boss
- Career must be consistent with family/Christian principles/living
- Family: wife and son
- Fitness
- Action

He used different tools of discovery programs to figure out who he is, what gives him energy and fulfillment, and where he can add value. He now needed to figure out the detail on each of his elements, so he hired a coach to help him through the process. Working with another believer going through the same process helped him to see how they live out their life.

Living God's Plan

The friend who had to leave his posting in China shook LZ. It's getting more challenging to have a long-term sustainable platform in China, so he treasures even more the opportunity to serve in the place he feels called to. Now, he is continuing the DNA process to figure out what is next for him.

Transformation Story: Should I Stay or Should I Go?

Renée (name changed) was a life insurance expert working in a top investment bank. She was strongly considering leaving the bank and joining an insurance company as a global leader. However, she had built credibility at the bank and was being considered for a promotion. She was torn: Should she stay, or should she go?

Through the DNA® process, she identified these key elements:

- Work in financial institutions, investment banking, or insurance
- Lead a large team
- Bring people together
- Influence people to follow her
- International experience
- Work with the top global clients
- English language fluency
- Trusted advisor to influential c-level executives

- Have an impact on their business

- Commercially savvy

- See things/opportunities others don't

- Like winning business

- Personal

- Family: husband and two children

- Arts

- Athletics: marathon runner

Given these elements, Renée saw that both options offered opportunities to use her gifts in different ways. Ultimately, she decided that staying with her current investment bank would allow her to engage more of her elements such as leading a large team and impacting c-level executives.

STEP 3 - DNA® ACTION

Small Steps Are Key

Bob Wiley and Dr. Leo Marvin had a rather strange doctor-patient relationship. You may remember them from the movie *What About Bob?* Bob, played by actor Bill Murray, is a disturbed individual with several different phobias who feels he has made a connection with Dr. Marvin. He really believes that Dr. Marvin will be able to solve his problems.

Bob wants Dr. Marvin to solve his issues immediately, but that is not what happens. As Bob sits in the chair in Dr. Marvin's office, Dr. Marvin walks over, hands him a book and tells him to take "baby steps." Baby steps out of the office. Baby steps down the hall. Baby steps onto the elevator. In other words, the path to Bob's freedom wasn't going to be found in an overnight, radical change, but through simple, obedient, small steps that would eventually lead to great change.

That is often how change happens in life and it most certainly is the experience of many in Scripture.

Instructions from Scripture: Small Steps of Faith

In the garden, Adam and Eve were not going to turn the Garden of God (Genesis 1–2) into the City of God (Revelation 21) overnight. It was going to happen through faithful, obedient, small steps.

When God calls Abraham to go to a new land (Genesis 12), God does not give him all the information at once. He calls Abraham to go to a land "that He would show him." In other words, Abraham was not going to get all the information he wanted on day one, but rather he was going to have to step out, trusting God along the journey.

When Jesus called the disciples to join Him in His mission, to enter into an entirely different purpose of life (fishers of men rather than fishers of fish), he didn't give them all the details but rather asked them to follow Him by faithful daily obedience.

For most of us, this is not easy to accept. We want it all now, all questions answered, all plans made, yet Scripture is clear that this is not how it works:

> The heart of man plans his way, but the LORD establishes his steps. (Proverbs 16:9)

> For I know the plans I have for you, declares the LORD, plans for welfare and not for evil, to give you a future and a hope. (Jeremiah 29:11)

> Come now, you who say, "Today or tomorrow we will go into such and such a town and spend a year there and trade and make a profit"—yet you do not know what tomorrow will bring… Instead you ought to say, "If the Lord wills, we will live and do this or that." (James 4:13–15)

There is one specific story in Scripture that really illustrates this point, and it is truly powerful. It is found in a little book in the Old Testament called Ruth. In the opening chapter, a husband, his wife (Naomi), and their two sons and their families leave the people of God and head out to the land of Moab. It is a time of famine, a time of cultural disobedience to the things of God, and this family decides to leave town.

While they are in Moab, both Naomi's husband and her two sons die. She is completely hopeless. When she decides to go back home, she tells her daughters-in-law to stay, for she has nothing to give them (keep in mind that in the Ancient Near East having no family meant having no hope). But Ruth, one of Naomi's daughters-in-law, returns with her.

When they return home, Naomi is bitter, angry, and without direction in life. But Ruth does something that will forever change their life. Which is what, praying until God sends down bread from heaven, solving their problems forever? No. Starting a Bible study from which a new ministry is born? No. It is actually something even more spiritual than that. Here is how the Bible puts it: "So she set out and went and gleaned in the field after the reapers, and she happened to come to the part of the field belonging to Boaz, who was of the clan of Elimelech" (Ruth 2:3).

In short, Ruth took the small step of faith of going out into the field. It was scary, dangerous, with lots of uncertainty (she was after all a Moabite living in another country), but she took that little step. And that little step landed her in the field of Boaz who would redeem her and Naomi's story. It all started with a woman's courage to take a small step in the right direction!

Baby steps. Baby steps.

Take Action and Take Control

Do you feel overwhelmed? You are not alone. Many leaders experience a schedule, workload, and set of demands so full they feel like they can't breathe. In this overloaded work life, one can often feel like a victim.

Don't be a victim. Life is not fair. Complaining and doing nothing is just complaining. It will not change or improve the situation. This can make you feel like a victim.

Instead, gain control. Taking the small steps, enjoying the process, and achieving small victories will show you that you can start to gain control over your life, career, health, finances, etc.

Small steps matter

In their book *The Power of Full Engagement,* James Loehr and Tony Schwartz explain, "Because change requires moving beyond our comfort zone, it is best initiated in small and manageable increments."

We don't take baby steps because we are afraid or incapable of achieving great things but because real change takes time to implement and integrate into a new normal.

The sense of forward motion is powerful

In his book *Smartcuts,* Shane Snow writes about the power of the "Big Mo" (momentum) in getting out of a rut:

> Harvard Business School professor Teresa Amabile has found that the answer is simply progress. A sense of forward motion. Regardless how small. Amabile found that minor victories at work were nearly as psychologically powerful as major breakthroughs. And momentum isn't just a powerful ingredient of success. It's also a powerful predictor of success.

Enjoy the moment, enjoy the process

In his book, *#NOW,* Dr. Max McKeown introduces the concept of being a "Nowist":

> In a Nowist mindset it seems better to enjoy the moment while doing something that you value than to do something just to impress other people. And this leads to some curious, surprising moments of clarity and enlightenment: If work can be enjoyed, then it doesn't need to be avoided. And if enjoyment is included as part of your valued goals, then joy is not a distraction.

> So, instead of getting stuck regretting the past, fearing the future or being paralyzed by trying to find the perfect plan, successful happy people actively change the future by taking action today.

They don't spend time figuring out the one most important thing. Instead, they instinctively do the next positive thing. They keep moving. They look while leaping and leap while looking. They don't get hung up on getting everything right, but on making a start and making things happen.

Seeing life as being about creatively connecting streams of action makes it easier to absorb the energy of unwelcome shocks or less dramatic setbacks. So that when you can't succeed the way you'd originally intended, you are able to slip into one of your other streams of action or replace one method or means to an end with something quite different.

A Nowist doesn't just take baby steps or build momentum, they build momentum around positive things so that they develop resilience when the unavoidable bumps happen along the way.

We tend to think in absolute terms: We either have no control (victim) or we have total control (a fallacy). We should instead think in relative terms. Spending one more dinner a week with our family is an improvement. Going home a little earlier on Thursday night is a joy. We should appreciate these small yet important victories. When we think this way, we actually gain more control over our schedule than we think.

Break down your goal/plan into smaller, bite size steps

Start down the path of more control by taking small yet important steps. Clarify specifically who and what is important to you. Then plan and move in the right direction. It's the small steps that matter. Don't be a victim!

My friends and I on the tennis team constantly joke (but also half seriously) about "Big Mo." Momentum is not only important in sports; it is also critical in life. How do you get into the "Big Mo" flow? In tennis, focus on and win the next point. This can lead to a string of points and then the win. In life, it's getting off your seat and moving forward.

In the iconic words of Lance's former employer, "Just do it."

Dr. McKeown (the Nowist) suggests,

> To make it easier to start, Nowists are better able to make the future feel like now. And because it is easier to be motivated to start when the deadline is closer, they use Nowist mind tricks to make the task deadline seem like part of the present. The desire to start immediately, despite the possibility of inefficiency, is a tendency that's been labeled pre-crastination.

The character of Forrester in the movie *Finding Forrester* mentors his student to "Write from your heart, edit with your head." If you are anything like me, it's not so easy to sit down and write chapters for a book, an important email, or succinct but clever blogs. What Sean Connery's character Forrester taught me about writing is to first write from the heart. Don't think, don't judge, just write. This is a wonderful technique because it gets you started. And we all know how difficult it is to start things. When we worry or think too much about how it sounds or how clear it is, we can get paralysis.

The most important step is the next one.

Then it's time to use your head to edit. Make the message clearer, choose the right words, adjust the tone, ensure it's focused, etc. It's easier to edit than create.

The most important step is the next one.

Make some linguistic adjustments

In his book *The Achievement Habit*, Bernard Roth suggests several linguistic tweaks that can make you more successful. Here are two to apply into your life:

Swap out *but* for *and*

When we are faced with two seemingly conflicting alternatives such as wanting to go out with friends or studying, we may say, "I want to go out with my friends, but I have to study tonight." Instead, Roth suggests saying, "I want to go out with my friends, and I have studying to do."

He writes: "When you use the word *but*, you create a conflict (and sometimes a reason) for yourself that does not really exist." In other words, it's possible to go out with your friends as well as study—you just need to find a solution.

Meanwhile, when you use the word *and*, "your brain gets to consider how it can deal with both parts of the sentence," Roth writes.

Swap out *have to* for *want to*

"This exercise is very effective in getting people to realize that what they do in their lives—even the things they find unpleasant—are in fact what they have chosen," he says.

Roth goes on to explain,

> Both of these tweaks are based on a key component of a problem-solving strategy called design thinking. When you employ this strategy, you try to challenge your automatic thinking and see things as they really are. When you experiment with different language, you may realize that a problem isn't as unsolvable as it seems, and that you have more control over your life than you previously believed.

Leverage Parkinson's Law

Many of us are prisoners to what's urgent, often ignoring what and who is important to us. This is where Parkinson's Law applies. If you can learn to apply this law into your career and life, you will begin to get control over it.

Parkinson's Law states that "Work expands to fill the time available to complete it." If you were given two weeks to complete a task the results would be the same if you were given three weeks to complete the same task. Work expands to fill the time to complete it. You would think given 50% more time to complete it, would generate 50% better results. But, it doesn't.

Apply this law to your life to "get a life." Let's say on average you work 70 hours a week. If you worked two fewer hours, would you see a significant reduction in your output? No. But if you spent two more hours with someone you love or on yourself, it would make a big difference. You're simply shifting two hours from where it makes no difference to where it will have a significant impact. That's leverage.

How to find those two hours? Actually there's no need. Considering Parkinson's Law, the best way is to just take them.

Try an experiment: This week, go home early one day or come in late one morning. Parkinson's Law dictates that you will naturally deliver the results you need to deliver even though you've given yourself less time. At the end of the week, analyze if your results suffered at all. Did anyone notice it?

I've worked with person after person on this technique and each has reported back the same thing. No reduction in results. No one seems to care or notice. They feel more refreshed and in more control over their schedule.

How to Take Small Steps

Let's start moving down the path. Open the Dream and Achieve Workbook, Step 3: Action worksheet.

The Step 3: Action worksheet cells B16–58 will fill in automatically from your Step 2: Drill Down worksheet. Follow these instructions to fill out the worksheet:

Fill in the yellow shaded boxes.

1. In column C, fill in actions you can do during the next **three months** to get more of your elements (column B) into your life right now and get you closer to your dream.

2. In column E, fill in actions you can do during the next **three days** to get more of your elements into your life right now and get you closer to your dream.

3. Now go to your calendar and schedule the three-day action plans from column E.

You don't have to accomplish all the three-day action plans at once. You need to keep going back to the plan to schedule subsequent three-day actions. The point is to move, continually and gradually.

Lance Tanaka Transformation: Action

Take a look at my 3-month, 3-day action plans. None of these action plans are urgent. Life will not stop if I don't do them. No one will yell at me for not doing them. However, each action plan in and of itself is important. This is when we need to develop a discipline to stay on track and execute these action plans, step by step. Remember: Small steps matter. Work your garden and reap the rewards of your efforts.

		Actions you can do during the next 3 **months**	Actions you can do during the next 3 **days**
	Highly influential: be the "go to" impact person		
who	Work with people I enjoy & the influential	Design leadership/management/communication products	Do a product list
what	Establish a co.	Target prospective clients I like and can impact	Compile the prospect list and start making connections
where	1. Greater China	Read books on China business culture	Compile a China book list today and read 1 book per month
when	By 2001	Work on my company business plan	Do business plan 1st draft

		Actions you can do during the next 3 **months**	Actions you can do during the next 3 **days**
Develop, mentor and influence			
who	Matt, Michael, bus execs, young pros, students, disciples	Spend 1-on-1 time with both sons	Set a weekly activity with each son
what	Motivate people to take action, leverage people open up to me	Develop a coaching program for each demographic	Develop a 1st draft program for leadership
where	Home, companies, associations, public venues, media, church	Formalize my EQ/motivation gift into a methodology	Develop a new habits methodology
when	Daily	Gain an understanding of social media	Set up a LinkedIn account

		Actions you can do during the next 3 **months**	Actions you can do during the next 3 **days**
Performing on stage			
who	Professionals, church, public	Look for internal public speaking opportunities	Talk to Head of Region to do internal co. presentations
what	Seminars, speeches, workshops, church lead worship	Work with 1-2 churches to lead the music 1-2 per month	Talk with Pastors at FCC & ECC
where	Companies, associations, public venues, media, churches	Do free external workshops in associations to test in leadership/management/communication	Contact HR Forum, CEO Forum, Amcham to do free workshops
when	Weekly	Do free DNA workshops for church organizations	Talk with Pastors at FCC & ECC

		Actions you can do during the next 3 **months**	Actions you can do during the next 3 **days**
Help people discover & leverage their gifting			
who	Christian leaders and secular leaders	Establish a DNA Foundation for believers & seekers	Do a first draft plan & network with potential DNA coaches
what	Set up a DNA foundation	Establish a prospect list	Talk with Pastors at FCC & ECC
where	China & US	Locate a partner	Talk with network to recruit a partner
when	Next career		

		Actions you can do during the next 3 **months**	Actions you can do during the next 3 **days**
Finance			
goal	Hit __ net worth target to retire in 2001	Develop a 10 year financial plan	Load Quickbooks retirement app
goal	Dream home in US	Develop a list of desired attributes for our US home	Research different US regions

	Actions you can do during the next 3 **months**	Actions you can do during the next 3 **days**
Health		
priority Maintain weight: don't gain beyond 1 lb.	Design an input (diet) and output (exercise) program	Start immediately
priority Look good naturally	Develop an integrated program of diet/fitness/self-discovery	Test the DNA self-discovery approach on me

	Actions you can do during the next 3 **months**	Actions you can do during the next 3 **days**
Relationships		
priority The Lord	Establish the DNA Foundation/read the New Testament in 1 yr	Read 1 chapter of the Bible daily
priority Renee, my wife	Show more empathy, patience	Set a date night weekly
priority Matt & Michael, my sons	Spend 1-on-1 time with both sons	Set a weekly activity with each son
missing Close circle of friends	Have regular contact	Start with Rob
repair Sister	Re-establish a relationship	Make a phone call

Transformation Story: Mike Burns from Corporate U.S. to Small-Business China

Nudge

Ever since going on a trip to the mainland in 1994, God has been nudging Mike Burns to build his platform in China. There he met his lifetime partner, Jill. As he was leaving the trip, he had a strong sense the Lord wanted him to return to China and to spend the rest of his life with Jill. She had the same two senses. What a confirmation!

Discovery

Since getting involved in ministry in college, Mike actively worked to discover God's plan. He tried many different types of ministry as well as assessment tools to discover his gifts of shepherding and leadership.

At Brady Corporation, he had a self-discovery breakthrough: Strategy and coaching were his strengths. This "ah-hah" moment gave him the vision to combine these strengths with his ministry gifts.

Action

Mike lived a life of obedience to continue tending his garden. He worked with Lance on a weekly basis to develop his coaching skills. On his knees he asked the Lord for help, to bring the right people into his life.

Both Jill and Mike were in lock step as partners to tolerate the risks and make their leap of faith.

Living God's Plan

It was clear to Mike and Jill, God wanted them to build their platform in China to minister to people from all over the world.

Slowly, the Lord opened doors to Mike. He moved from the corporate world of Walmart logistics to General Electric P&L leadership roles to Erico China General Manager and finally to Brady Corporation Director of Sales and Marketing Asia Pacific. Each of his job transitions were guided by a desire to maintain his time with his family as a priority or get to and stay in China, even though many times, his employers wanted him back in the U.S.

As his and Jill's impact took off in China through their fitness business, they realized their call to a lifetime of ministry was to utilize their China platform of business to impact and shepherd people.

Although it took 13 years to get back to China, he eventually made his way there and established a life of impact and purpose. Looking back on his journey, Mike realized it was more of God waiting on him, not him waiting on God.

Transformation Story: Howard Abe finding God Out of Personal Tragedy

Nudge

Howard Abe enjoyed management consulting. He was making good money and achieved what many consultants aspired to: becoming partner. Although things on the outside seemed to fall into place, inside he felt that his personal life was increasingly spinning out of control. His wake-up call was a troubled marriage. Always traveling on the road, he was slow to pick up on his wife's unhappiness. He sought advice from his colleagues in the firm, but sadly, troubled marriages were all too common. His wife decided to leave after ten years of marriage and they divorced. He didn't see it coming, so it really hit him hard.

Discovery

Howard had stayed away from church for many years but decided to return after being invited by a friend. Realizing he was like the prodigal son who had abandoned his loving Father, he rededicated his life to Christ. In his discovery process, Howard realized his identity was driven by consulting success, financial reward, and recognition from colleagues and clients. God began working on his heart and opened his eyes to an unconditional love and a greater purpose he had never known before. Over several years, Howard experienced an inward transformation and the joy of putting God at the center of his identity, building authentic relationships, and serving others both in the church and on overseas mission trips.

Actions

No longer feeling in stride with the career he had poured himself into, he began to earnestly seek the Lord in prayer. He reached out to colleagues but found that they could not relate to his struggle since they were all running on the same professional treadmill. He talked with close Christian friends in the church and even his pastor. Without a clear direction, but knowing the status quo wouldn't lead to an answer, Howard took a one-year sabbatical and studied theology in the idyllic setting of Oxford, UK. His relationship and trust in God continued to strengthen while he was away from a busy work environment, surrounded by those who were also in pursuit of God's plans.

Living God's Plan

On the career front, following his sabbatical, Howard prayed about several new job leads but decided to return to work at the consulting firm. It was a confusing one-year of discerning and waiting on God's plans and feeling like a fish out of water in a culture where he had once thrived.

Everything changed when Howard received an unexpected call from Ravi Zacharias International Ministries (RZIM) to meet and explore a new opportunity. God orchestrated a once-in-a-lifetime opportunity to serve a global ministry in a leadership role with a fresh mission of encouraging leaders and influencers to know the same God who had changed his own life.

On the personal front, God's plans and perfect timing had already been unfolding through a new special relationship. Howard and Olivia had met at church and dated for more than a year before they were married. Although Howard felt that he didn't deserve a second chance at a lifetime partner, God's plans were more than he could have ever imagined. Howard and Olivia have been blessed with two beautiful children.

The transition from consulting to ministry as well as new family life was a big hurdle. However, with Olivia's full support, Howard knew that this was the sign from God that it was the right door to walk through. He became the Executive Director Asia Pacific at RZIM and felt right at home where the mission, people, and culture resonated with his passion for pioneering, impact, and excellence.

Develop New Habits

"Could you make those kids be quiet?" He didn't say it; but that's what he was thinking. Stephen Covey, in his book *7 Habits of Highly-Effective People*, tells about a Sunday morning subway ride in New York City. Everyone was sitting quietly: one person reading the newspaper, another lost in thought, another resting against the wall. Everything was peaceful.

Then a man and his children walked onto the subway. The children were loud and rambunctious—throwing things, yelling, and messing with other people's stuff. And what made the situation worse was the man did absolutely nothing. He just sat there with his head in his hands, looking at the floor. It was one of those moments when everyone starts making eye contact and they are all thinking, "Seriously, get control of your kids!"

This went on for several minutes, until Stephen had enough. He turned to the man, and said, "Sir, your children are disturbing a lot of people. Do you think you could do something?" The man lifted his head, as though waking up from a nap, and said, "I'm sorry. I should do something. We just left the hospital about an hour ago where their mother, my wife, died. We're not sure how to handle all of this."

Covey writes, "Can you imagine how I felt in that moment? My paradigm shifted. Suddenly I saw things in a completely different way. My irritation vanished. My heart, once full of frustration, was now full of compassion. Everything about my situation changed."

Most of us can relate to a situation like that. I don't mean where we had to open mouth and insert foot (though I'm sure that's true, too)! I'm talking about when you were convinced you knew reality, exactly what was going on, had everything figured out, but then something or someone came along and changed your whole perspective.

> *Convinced marriage wasn't for you…then he/she came along.*
>
> *Convinced they had lots of life left…then the test results came back.*
>
> *Convinced you could never love anything more…then she was born.*
>
> *Convinced marriage was forever…then he said, "We need to talk."*
>
> *Convinced Christianity was for others…then "Jesus changed your life."*

All of us can relate to a time when we thought we knew reality but were forced to experience change. What would have seemed to be unthinkable is now a reality.

Change is something that is not always easy to accept. It's not pleasant to learn that maybe we need a different perspective on reality. History is full of examples of people unable to imagine things changing. Consider how these statements look in hindsight:

"There is no reason anyone would want
a computer in their home."

—Ken Olsen, Digital Equipment Corp., 1977

"The 'telephone' has too many shortcomings to be
seriously considered as a means of communication.
The device is inherently of no value to us."

—Western Union memo, 1876

"The television won't be able to hold any market
after the first six months. People will get tired
of staring at a plywood box every night."

—Darryl Zanuck, 1946

"The horse is here to stay, the automobile is only a novelty."

—President of Michigan Savings Bank, 1903

"Everything that can be invented has been invented."

—Charles Duell, officer of the U.S. of Patents, 1899

Now, it is easy to laugh at these examples, but we do the same thing. We look at our reality and often think it will never be any different. Yet, in order for us to fully embrace the mission and purpose of God for our life, we *must* embrace change. Responding to that nudge leads you to *make a change*. Going through the discovery process *changes* the way you understand yourself, and taking action *creates change* in your life.

Instructions from Scripture: Prepare for the New Mission

In Acts 10, God takes two men and a mission and institutes change that would have been very hard to imagine. Peter has been doing ministry for Jesus, and he is tired and hungry, so he goes to pray on the roof of the house where he is staying. As he prays, he falls asleep (you thought you were the only one who did this!). While he sleeps, he has a dream about a large sheet stretching across the four corners of the earth with all sorts of animals, reptiles, and birds. Peter is told to "take and eat."

For most of us, that would not be a problem, but it was kind of a big deal for Peter. That's because the animals in this dream were forbidden in the Torah; eating food like this went against everything he had learned about being faithful to God. But God was calling Peter into an entirely different way of living. God was doing a new work in Peter's life, and Peter would have to change the way he thought in order to embrace this new change.

In fact, in this specific example, God is preparing Peter for more than a new diet; he is preparing Peter for a new mission. You see, the reason that Jews like Peter were not allowed to eat certain foods was because those foods were associated with certain people—Gentiles. But in Acts 10, God commands Peter to embrace a small change because God was preparing Peter for large change. Eating the food was a small illustration of embracing the new mission of God, which would include both Jews and Gentiles alike.

This was hard for Peter. Very hard. But change was required in order to embrace this new mission. The truth is, when your life is focused on the mission and purpose of God you will be forced to embrace a level of change you once thought was unthinkable. You'll be friendly to the person of a different political stance, adopt a child of a different race, live in a neighborhood no one else wants to live in, give generously, forgive the person who hurt you, or embrace a new direction in life. Bottom line, if you don't like change, you won't like the mission and purpose of God for your life.

After all, isn't the Christian life from beginning to end about change?

> Therefore, if anyone is in Christ, he is a new creation. The old has passed away; behold, the new has come. (2 Cor 5:17)

> Not that I have already obtained this or am already perfect, but I press on to make it my own, because Christ Jesus has made me his own. Brothers, I do not consider that I have made it my own.

But one thing I do: forgetting what lies behind and straining forward to what lies ahead, I press on toward the goal for the prize of the upward call of God in Christ Jesus. Let those of us who are mature think this way, and if in anything you think otherwise, God will reveal that also to you. (Phil 3:12–15)

Behold! I tell you a mystery. We shall not all sleep, but we shall all be changed, in a moment, in the twinkling of an eye, at the last trumpet. For the trumpet will sound, and the dead will be raised imperishable, and we shall be changed. (1 Cor 15:51–52)

If you don't like change, if you are not willing to embrace change, if you are not ready to view life entirely different, you will struggle to discover the purpose and mission God has for you.

Are you like Stephen Covey on that subway? Certain you have reality figured out? Unwilling to accept that maybe there is a different perspective you need? Are you like Peter, unwilling to embrace a new idea or path in life? The truth is, God has a purpose for you. A mission in life. And that purpose and mission will require embracing a new way of living…

MBTAM: A Framework for Building New Habits and Changing Your Life

Over years of helping people change, I've discovered, modified, and developed a framework that is practical and highly effective in breaking any bad habit or creating a new one. It's called MBTAM. I use it in just about every coaching engagement. The MBTAM framework works because it sets out precise action plans in bite-sized, easy-to-implement steps that are realistic and achievable.

"MBTAM" may not be the most eloquent acronym, but we're focused on results, not being cute. In brief, the acronym stands for:

Motivation

Behaviors that are precise

Timing that's specific

Achievable targets

Measurement

Parts of the MBTAM framework draw together aspects of the other principles, but as we describe how to deploy it to structure behavioral change, you will see why we list it as its own principle.

Motivation

We begin with motivation because it is the foundation for any movement, change, or improvement. It provides the energy needed for change.

Change is hard, even though it may be clear and simple. The way you think, feel, and behave—essentially, your habits of being—are already hard-wired into your brain. Thus, changing your habits requires you to rewire your brain. Therefore, you must really, really want to change.

In *A User's Guide to the Brain*, Dr. John Ratey writes,

> The brain is not a neatly organized system. It is often compared to an overgrown jungle of 100 billion nerve cells, or neurons. [. . .] The neuron and its thousands of neighbors send out roots and branches—the axons and dendrites—in all directions, which intertwine to form an interconnected tangle with 100 trillion constantly changing connections. The connections guide our bodies and behaviors, even as every thought and action we take physically modifies their patterns.

Our neurons are constantly competing to make connections and these connections are what make us who we are.

But our brains are very efficient. As Dr. Ratey goes on to say, "Connections that aren't used are eventually pruned. [. . .] Neurons that survive communicate rapid-fire across the synapses. The more firing that occurs across a specific connection, the stronger that pathway becomes. [. . .] Circuit connections are made stronger or weaker throughout a lifetime according to use." In other words, we must link the change we want to our motivation if we're going to overcome our own neural wiring.

Behaviors

You need to define your new habit in terms of a precise behavior. The more precise the better.

Precise behaviors . . .

- Are clear

- Are easier to influence

- Are actionable

- Are easier to measure (it's clear if you performed them or not)

- Lead to attitude change when performed consistently over time

By specifying precise behaviors, you create practical actions you can take on a regular basis, what Loehr and Schwartz call Positive Rituals: "A broad and persuasive array of studies confirms that specificity of timing and precision of behavior dramatically increase the likelihood of success."

Define your desired change into as precise a behavior as possible. We have a tendency to define the change in "imprecise" ways. We need to make sure it is clear, observable, and measurable.

Imprecise	Precise
Listen better	• Stop interrupting people. • Affirm what a person says before I speak.
Spend more time developing my people	• Have a developmental conversation with a staff member. • At the start of a project, ask each team member what s/he wants to get out of it
Take more initiative	• When reporting an issue to my boss, I will present options that address the problem and offer my recommendation

Lance Tanaka Transformation: Developing New Habits

Intending to exercise more next week is so imprecise that it is difficult to schedule or measure and probably will lead to failure. Let me give you an example of how I define my exercise behaviors:

A minimum of 30 minutes or 5 kilometers of running

Tennis: If it's doubles, 2 hours. If it's singles, 1 hour.

Baseball: 1 game

Weightlifting: 25 minutes

Hiking: 1 hour

Anything less than these definitions does not count as exercise. This precise definition is highly actionable, measurable, and schedulable.

Timing

As I've described above, precise behaviors can be scheduled. Specific timing and scheduling is an essential part of behavior change. We have so many things that keep us busy. If we do not schedule the time for what is important to us, less important things will interrupt us and take over the whole day. You need to set a specific time you will do the new precise behavior. The more specific the better.

How likely are you to accomplish some goal you set for next week? If you are very motivated, maybe the odds are good, but for most of us they are poor.

How much more likely could you accomplish that task next Monday, which is more specific? What about next Monday at 8 a.m.? I think you get the picture.

Be very clear about when you will perform an action. It should be so clear you can schedule it in a calendar.

You also need to have a contingency plan in case you don't do it as scheduled. If you can't do it on Monday at 8 a.m. because you suddenly need to take a trip, reschedule it for Tuesday at 8 a.m.

Achievable targets

Define behaviors and times that you can actually achieve. Set yourself up for success.

Remember Loehr and Schwartz's "manageable increments." When we set an aggressive behavior target, we may achieve it in the first week, but in the second week it tends to drop off. And by the third week it drops even further to zero. The fourth week ends up in another zero and so on. This is a good reason why dieting doesn't seem to last.

It may feel counter-intuitive, but I'm going to ask you to do something that you are rarely ever told to do: Set the bar low! The mindset, "I will do my best" is not good enough. The mindset must be, "I will do it, no matter what, no excuses." So, it better be something you can actually do.

In the beginning, you will look for all kinds of reasons not to do it: "I'm too tired," "I have a lot of work to do." Therefore, you must force yourself to do it. That's why setting a low bar is more realistic and practical.

Scientists tell us—and this has been verified by us in thousands of cases—that if you force yourself to do a new behavior over a 3–4-week period, it will start rewiring the brain. It will become easier and more natural.

Measurement

If you want someone to do something, you must measure whether they did it or not. Measurement doesn't necessarily have to be empirical. It can be simply asking if they did it. Either way, it must be measured.

The *law of effect* is a psychological principle, advanced in 1905 by Edward Thorndike, which states that "responses that produce a satisfying effect in a particular situation become more likely to occur again in that situation."

Quite simply, if you get rewarded for doing something, you will do it again.

People do what you measure. Why do people in a company constantly focus on sales? Because the company measures it annually, quarterly, monthly, weekly, daily, and in some cases hourly. Of course, people will be focused on it!

Simply set a target and a system to measure how often you achieve it.

Transformation Story: Going Home for Dinner

A workaholic partner in a Big 4 accounting company in China was struggling with work-life balance. Her brain was wired for goal achievement, excellence, long hours—like I said, a workaholic. She was having problems at home, for she rarely had dinner at home with her husband and son during the week.

When I asked what her plan was to improve this, she said, "I will go home more often for dinner." I knew this was too vague and lacked specificity, so I asked, "Is it working?" Unsurprisingly, she said, "No."

After a little discussion about MBTAM, she decided she would go home for dinner three times a week.

I asked her, "Can you do this every week?"

"I can't do it when I have one of those tough weeks," she answered.

"How often do you have these tough weeks?" I asked.

"Seems like nearly every week," was her reply.

So, I told her, "I realize you desire to have dinner with the family three times a week, but let's experiment with trying to do one. Can you do this every week?"

She said, "Yes, that's very reasonable and doable."

We set the bar low, and suddenly the goal became highly achievable.

She set the target for every Thursday night at 6 p.m. She also had a contingency. If she had to travel on Thursday night, she would set an alternate night for that week.

She then wrote on her calendar for this Thursday to go home at 6. That first Thursday night, she had to concentrate and remind herself all day long, "I'm going home at 6, I'm going home at 6."

That may sound silly, but here's the point: *She did it!*

The next week, she wrote in the calendar, "Go home at 6." That day she again had to keep reminding herself to go home. She did it and found that it was easier than the first Thursday had been.

After a while she found she did not have to remind herself, and a few weeks later she did not even have to write it in the calendar. *It became a habit.* The amazing thing is that her colleagues—including her boss—worked around it.

In order to sustain the momentum, she set up a simple measurement system. She set a minimum target of three Thursdays per month. Every month, she would plan out in advance on which three Thursdays she would go home at 6:00. Then she kept a running total of successful months.

Being able to create a new good habit and get more control over her schedule and her life made her feel great. She has since increased her MBTAM to not working on Sunday.

> *Let's continue down the path. Go to the Dream and Achieve Workbook,*
> *MBTAM worksheet*

Cells A11–B37 will fill in automatically from your STEP 3: Action worksheet.

1. Fill in the yellow shaded boxes and use the drop-down boxes for direction to bring more of your elements into your daily life.

2. Fill in your precise behaviors in column D and specific timing in column F. Now you need to ask yourself, "Is this precise behavior and specific timing really achievable? Is your mindset, "I will do it, no matter what, no excuses"? If not, you need to reduce the timing and behavior.

Move Down the Path

One of the popular bands when I (Wes) was growing up was a band name Van Halen. Like every band, when Van Halen was hired to play a show, they provided a contract that outlined specific things the promoter would be responsible for—things like sound and lighting requirements, backstage setup, security needs, and so on.

Well, there was on odd request that Van Halen put in their contact which has become known as the "M&M rider." Under the "Munchies" section of the contract, they list this item: "M&M's (WARNING: ABSOLUTELY NO BROWN ONES)." At first, you might think that the band's fame had gone to their heads, but they had a practical reason for this clause.

You see, the band did hundreds of shows every year with a complex setup (trailers full of gear, equipment, etc.), so it was important for the contract to be followed exactly as stated. As a result, the band had the "no brown M&M's" request in the contract to gauge if the contract had been followed closely. If they arrived at a show, walked backstage to the dressing room, and noticed brown M&M's, they knew the contract had not been taken seriously and would demand a check of the entire setup. In other words, even though something like "no brown M&M's" seemed so small and insignificant, it actually was very important and could not be overlooked.

I think that example is often true in life. Namely, we tend to neglect the "little things" that actually matter in big ways. The truth is, the little things matter. Let me explain. When we think about our vocations and careers we tend to only think of the "big items": How much money will I make? Will I have the title I want? What kind of lifestyle will I have? We may end up neglected the "little things": Will this keep me from being intentional with my kids? Will I have time for the hobbies I enjoy? Just like it would be easy to ignore "brown M&M's" in order to take care of the bigger things (sound equipment and lighting), we ignore the seemingly lesser things and make decisions based on only a few criteria. The reality is, until we find balance, we won't find satisfaction.

Instructions from Scripture: The Little Things Matter

> One who is faithful in a very little is also faithful in much, and one who is dishonest in a very little is also dishonest in much. (Luke 16:10)

> He put another parable before them, saying, "The kingdom of heaven is like a grain of mustard seed that a man took and sowed in his field. It is the smallest of all seeds, but when it has grown it is larger than all the garden plants and becomes a tree, so that the birds of the air come and make nests in its branches." (Matthew 13:31–32)

Passages like those above should not be taken out of context. For example, in Matthew 13, Jesus is talking about the kingdom of God and how it isn't always easy to see ("small seeds"), but it is growing all around you and will one day consume creation.

That said, there is a principle taught here that is practical to life, namely, how we often neglect the little things that have a huge impact. Just like it is easy to dismiss the kingdom of God for seemingly more "urgent" things in life, we can neglect the things that appear small yet have great significance. But just like ignoring the "brown M&M's" was a sign of a bigger problem, so too is neglecting the seemingly lesser things in life.

As you work through the DNA exercise, you are discovering multiple areas of your life that matter, and all of these things are a part of your garden. Therefore, you cannot neglect any of them if you want to be both obedient to

God and satisfied in life. If you only make decisions on "big items" (money, fame, status, lifestyle) and ignore the "smaller things" (time, relationships, fun) your life will not be balanced and you will not faithfully tend your garden.

Use Your Elements to Guide Your Decisions

To start making better life and career decisions, we will use the Dream and Achieve Workbook, Career Choice worksheet.

Cells B15–58 automatically fill from your STEP 2: Drill Down worksheet.

1. Fill in yellow shaded boxes.

2. When faced with difficult decisions, imagine your options in D13-J13.

3. Evaluate each option by your elements in column B, rank 1–5 in each box, 5 being the highest.

4. Highlight the boxes with the highest rating amongst the options for each element

5. Print it out and see which options give you most of your key elements

Lance Tanaka Transformation: Decision Criteria

After completing this exercise, starting my own company (option 4) received the highest score (4.4; see cell J60 in the example worksheet). Also, looking at the red boxes, option four , starting my own company was the pretty obvious choice.

In some of your cases, the options may not be as clear as my situation, but it does give you a better idea. It may also allow you to throw out a more obvious option. This process is helpful because it puts all of your most important criteria for your life and career in one place.

Wes Feltner Transformation: Decision Criteria

As I felt God's nudging to start Lead Well Ministries, the most important criterion was the feeling I could make a larger impact through this transition than remaining in a local church. Freedom was an important piece for me, as I wanted the ability to exercise my gifting and my passion in multiple ways as God opened more and more opportunities. Legacy was another important part for me; rather than serving in contexts with a long history of other great leaders, I wanted to be able to do something on my own to leave a legacy for the gospel and for my children as well.

It's a Process

The approach to finding your purpose/God's plan is in one sense actually quite simple. Unfortunately, it's difficult for some people because it doesn't come as some revelation from the sky. Rather, this journey requires a lifestyle mindset shift.

As we've described in this book, tending your garden, nurturing your God-given gifts, requires that you understand some key principles:

- Being excited with North and the knowledge it brings.

- It is about moving (taking action) without knowing the answer (True North).

- It's a leap of faith that the Lord will bless our journey wherever it takes us with the decisions we make.

- We need to forge a discipline to persevere, even when things don't seem to be working out or the people around us tell us we're crazy.

- It's also about reading the people He puts in our path and recognizing the windows that are open to us.

This journey is a process.

In order to keep going, we need to link our journey to our motivations. Through the thousands of people we've coached, we've found that motivation is necessary for change and movement.

It also helps to find someone who can keep you on track, to hold you accountable.

Our purpose is to help you along the path. Please lean on us. We're here to help. It's our element.

Lance Tanaka Transformation: To be continued…

> Whoever accepts anyone I send accepts me and whoever accepts me accepts the one who sent me. (John 13:20)

I'm a Type A and have a tendency to rely on my own hard work and not on Him as the Chief. This can lead me down wasted paths, pursuing unsuccessful products and clients. During this journey, I had to learn to let the Lord lead. Near the beginning, I had to make decisions on which markets to focus on, not spreading my limited resources so thinly. China was not my initial primary focus (being Japanese is not the best nationality for gaining acceptance in China). However, the doors to clients in China opened up like the Red Sea. The Lord continually introduced people into my path that would lead to business there. It was apparent to me He wanted me in China.

So how do I now choose new markets and products? Instead of making extensive plans, I first pray and see what windows open. The windows tend to be people that He brings into my pathway. Now that I have a successful business in China, I'm sitting back and allowing him to lead me to the next markets. Who knows what's next? The U.S., SE Asia?

Darren Ho Transformation (*see Identify Your Strengths*): To be continued…

A few years into the self-discovery process, Darren realized that he could have a far greater impact on people beyond his company. He researched and took several assessment tools. He took the DNA® tool approach as a foundation to building his own process and created The Restored Leader where he could leverage his passion to help people on their journey to becoming authentic leaders, the kind people follow not because they have to but because they want to.

The Restored Leader coaches people to create a seamless fabric of leadership from home to community (church) and to work (the world). It may start in one place, but it needs to move through them all. He envisioned a future where every leader harnesses the power of their Core Values to thrive in their calling, resulting in thriving organizations.

The journey continues.

Howard Abe Transformation (*see Small Steps are Key*): To be continued…

God's plan continues to be revealed. Today, Howard is passionate about mentoring professionals and pointing them to Christ. He recently completed executive coaching training and launched into leadership coaching. Howard also helped to plant a new church alongside young families as a volunteer lay pastor, doing it all on an integrated basis with his RZIM work and family life. Howard describes his pursuit and journey as a dance with God. The more we give up control and trust God to take the lead, the more amazing and beautiful the dance becomes.

Mike Burns Transformation (*see Small Steps are Key*): To be continued…

Mike had two key supporters: me and his friend Jon. I affirmed he would be a great coach and provided a pathway to be a coach. Jon did the same regarding his consulting vision. We helped him navigate and make the big leap of faith to leave the comfort of the corporate world and become an entrepreneur and create Asia Global Solutions Ltd.

Prior to the move, his greatest fear was being able to financially live as an expat in China with three school-age kids. But relying on the Lord, he went out and marketed himself to potential coaching and consulting prospects. God affirmed his move of faith by giving him a big contract. People started approaching him. Another affirmation. God was his Marketing Director.

Now, Mike is at the stage in his journey to transition to actively do business development, expanding his platform and network.

Instructions from Scripture: It's Wrong to Do Nothing

"Oh, man, that guy just died." Those were the chilling words of a teenager as he and his friends stood at the edge of the water and watched a man drown. Jamel Dunn was a 32-yr-old disabled man who went swimming in a pond in Cocoa, FL. When he realized he had drifted too far, he cried for help to the teenagers on the bank. The teenagers not only didn't respond, they mocked him and recorded his final moments on their cell phone.

Jamel's body was discovered three days later. No one knew about the teenagers until the cellphone video surfaced on social media, causing public outrage followed by a police investigation. The police discovered, according to their report, "the kids were at the park and saw the man walk into the water. When he started to struggle and scream for help, they just laughed. They didn't call the police, call 911, tell anybody. They just stood there and laughed."

The kicker of it all was that, while their response was morally reprehensible, it was perfectly legal. You can go back to a famous legal case in the 1920's where a man fell off a pier and drowned while a sun-bather did nothing. The family filed suit. The state declared he had "no obligation to act."

Supreme Court Justice Anthony Kennedy, in a 2012 case said, "You don't have the duty to rescue someone if that person is in danger. If a blind man is walking in front of a car, you do not have the duty to stop him…while there may be severe moral criticisms, that's the law." When the mayor of Cocoa, FL, was asked to comment on Jamel's death, he said, "Never in my life would I have thought we would need a law to make someone take action."

The reason there was outrage over that situation is because we all know deep down that it is wrong to do nothing when it is your responsibility to do something! It is wrong to do nothing while an elderly person is taken advantage of. It is wrong to do nothing while a friend continues down a destructive path. There are times in life when you must take action, you must do something!

Throughout this "Tend Your Garden" process we've been giving you examples of the "nudge" that begins the process of moving you in the right direction. Take a moment to reflect and write down some of the nudges you've experienced through this process:

_____

_____

_____

_____

_____

What self-discoveries have you made? What new paths are you considering, what opportunities are you pursuing?

_____

_____

_____

_____

_____

James, the brother of Jesus, has strong words about people who fritter away today and put things off until tomorrow:

> Come now, you who say, "Today or tomorrow we will go into such and such a town and spend a year there and trade and make a profit"—yet you do not know what tomorrow will bring. What is your life? For you are a mist that appears for a little time and then vanishes. Instead you ought to say, "If the Lord wills, we will live and do this or that." As it is, you boast in your arrogance. All such boasting is evil. So whoever knows the right thing to do and fails to do it, for him it is sin. (James 4:13–17)

James is addressing people who are passively going about life. "Tomorrow I will do such and such or go to this place or that," they say, all the while assuming they have plenty of time. Nonsense! What is your life? It is like a vapor. It is here for a moment and then gone!

So, what is James's conclusion? "Whoever knows the right thing to do and fails to do it, for him *it is sin*." Wow. In other words, it is sin to do nothing when you know you should do something. It is sin to be passive when you have been called to action. This isn't the only time James speaks this way:

> What good is it, my brothers, if someone says he has faith but does not have works? Can that faith save him? If a brother or sister is poorly clothed and lacking in daily food, and one of you says to them, "Go in peace, be warmed and filled," without giving them the things needed for the body, what good is that? So also faith by itself, if it does not have works, is dead. (James 2:14–17)

> For if anyone is a hearer of the word and not a doer, he is like a man who looks intently at his natural face in a mirror. For he looks at himself and goes away and at once forgets what he was like. But the one who looks into the perfect law, the law of liberty, and perseveres, being no hearer who forgets but a doer who acts, he will be blessed in his doing. (James 1:23–25)

Did you catch the last part of verse 25? A *doer*, the one who *acts*, will be blessed in his or her doing! Do you want the blessing of God in your life? Then *do something!*

What are some of the action steps you have taken during this process or plan to take in the immediate future?

_____

_____

_____

_____

_____

On your "Tend Your Garden" journey, you have identified your passions and strengths, you've located your directional "north," you have gained a clearer understanding as to the garden you've been given to work. It is our desire to leave you with one simple but challenging thought: Whoever knows the right thing to do and fails to do it, for him (or her) it is sin.

It is now time to take action. To work your garden for the glory of God. No more excuses; it's time to execute. Baby steps? Yes. But steps nonetheless! Don't be the servant who buried his talent in the ground. Be the good and faithful servant in the garden of God.

It is our desire and prayer that, as you take action, you will be fruitful and multiple in many ways. That you will experience God and His blessings in ways you've never known. And just as Adam and Eve demonstrated God's goodness through their dominion over their garden, that you, too, will be a shining light of God's goodness in the world. God has given you one life. God has given you a specific garden. Identify it. Pursue it. Tend your Garden for the glory of God!

Testimonials

There are many books on Leadership and Faith, and yet Lance & Wes have managed to combine the two in a practical and action-oriented manual for those seeking to make a difference. If you are interested in flourishing at the intersection of God and Work, then this book and its principles are a must-read.

--Richard Jasper, Founding Partner Wealth Investment Partners LLC

I have had the pleasure of knowing Lance over the past fifteen years and have felt and seen his talent for helping people identify and channel their core strengths and passions to achieve their dreams. Lance can help you see the obvious, be honest with yourself and move your life toward where you really want it to be.

-- Mark Norbom, General Electric China President

In my two decades plus as a racetrack announcer, talk radio host and play-by-play broadcaster for the Minnesota Vikings, I have seen and endured a lot. Most of the amazing experiences have involved me frequently giving thanks to God for the wonderful professional existence he has provided me and all the unique people I have met. When I heard Pastor Wes Feltner teach, I experienced the Word in a way I never had experienced. Meeting Wes has better helped me sow seeds of faith on a daily basis and handle adversity and daily struggles in my life.

--Paul Allen, The Voice of the Minnesota Vikings

Lance's ability to channel his passion to his work has been a real inspiration. The techniques developed in this book have fundamentally changed the way

I work. Lance guided me to find a place where my strength and passion meet. I also learned to stop complaining but actively deal with the frustrations in daily work with a clear boundary. I can honestly say I have never felt happier or more fulfilled.

--Chao Xingjuan (Jane), Co-founder and CEO Ceribell Inc.

It is a pleasure to endorse Tend Your Garden, knowing the importance of pursuing and discovering one's purpose in life through lessons learned in two decades of founding and leading healthcare companies. Knowing Wes Feltner as a pastor and friend, I can't think of a better person to help teach us these lessons. Thank you, Wes for your leadership and generosity in sharing this gift with all of us.

--Kyle Rolfing Healthcare Entrepreneur

If you are looking to gain traction, motivation and focus to move towards your God-given purpose in life, drop everything and read this book! Lance is one of the top executive coaches in the world. He has helped thousands of leaders, (myself included), find their true meaning and then align their goals and activity around that meaning. His approach as an author mirrors his approach as a coach: authentic and practical! This is a must-read!

--Mike Burns, Managing Director Asia Growth Solutions Ltd.

Lance is a very passionate person. He concerns himself with both the people around him and the intricacies of life. Most people ask a very important question too late. "What do I want?" Lance not only discovers a very simple yet effective way of self-discovery, but he's also eager to share this special method with others hoping especially that young people would find it useful. Lance currently works with the young talents within my company on the special DNA process of self-discovery, I am able to witness how his approach can make a huge difference in others' lives.

--Elisa Wong, Hilti VP Human Resources - Asia Pacific

We all have dreams to build and stories to tell. To succeed in story-telling, one must construct a compelling story revolving around the journey of realizing one's dream. Lance's well articulated step by step approach is a practical guide that adds certainty to your personal plan as you transcribe your dream into a lifetime story.

--Joseph Tse, Deloitte Managing Partner Greater China

Lance is one of the very few people that influenced me fundamentally, helping me discover who I am and more importantly, who I want to be. I had faith in him and what he coached; he made me have faith in myself. He let me have wild dreams and empowered me to pursue them.

--Mavis Fu, Tsinghua University student

Not everyone can walk the talk and Lance is one who can. That's what makes Lance unique in his ability to help others realize their dreams. As a coach, he is not there to give you answers, but rather he is one of the best sparring partner, who ultimately brings you to self-realization to pursue your dreams.

--Gerald Tan, Daimler General Manager China & Lei Shing Hong Executive Director

References

Your Personal Garden Tools

Julio Diaz story taken from Story Corps, originally aired March 28, 2008, on NPR's Latino USA. https://storycorps.org/stories/julio-diaz/

Joshua Bell story: Gene Weingarten, "Pearls Before Breakfast: Can one of the nation's great musicians cut through the fog of a D.C. rush hour? Let's find out." *The Washington Post* Apr. 8, 2007. https://www.washingtonpost.com/

Don't Look for the "Answer"

Walter Houston story lightly adapted from "Man, 91, dies waiting for will of God," *Lark News* http://www.larknews.com/archives/202. Accessed March 20, 2020.

Marie Forleo, *Everything is Figureoutable*. Portfolio/Penguin, 2019.

Identify Your Passions

Bowerman article: Kenny Moore, "Track and Field's Master Teacher: One of his runners recalls the genius of Oregon coaching giant and Nike cofounder Bill Bowerman," *Sports Illustrated* Jan. 24, 2000. Accessed March 24, 2020. https://www.si.com/vault/2000/01/24/272677/track-and-fields-master-teacher-one-of-his-runners-recalls-the-genius-of-oregon-coaching-giant-and-nike-cofounder-bill-bowerman

King quote about sweeping streets from his speech to Baratt Junior High School in Philadelphia on October 26, 1967.

McKinsey leadership study: "The Value of Centered Leadership: McKinsey Global Survey Results," McKinsey & Co. October 2010. www.mckinsey.com.

James M. Kouzes, and Barry Z. Posner. *Learning Leadership: The Five Fundamentals of Becoming an Exemplary Leader*. Wiley, 2016.

Identify Your Strengths

Peter Flade, Jim Asplund, and Gwen Elliot. "Employees Who Use Their Strengths Outperform Those Who Don't." *Business Journal* (October 8, 2015).

Small Steps Are Key

On small steps leading to change: James E. Loehr and Tony Schwartz. *The Power of Full Engagement*. New York: Simon & Schuster, 2013.

On forward momentum and success: Shane Snow, *Smartcuts: How Hackers, Innovators, and Icons Accelerate Success*. Soundview Executive Book Summaries. October 2016.

On enjoying the moment: Max McKeown, *#Now: The Surprising Truth About the Power of Now*. Soundview Executive Book Summaries. November 2016.

On writing from the heart: Gus Van Zant, dir. *Finding Forrester*. Culver City, CA: Columbia Pictures, 2000.

On linguistic adjustments: Bernard Roth, *The Achievement Habit: Stop Wishing, Start Doing, and Take Command of Your Life*. New York: HarperCollins, 2015.

Develop New Habits

On paradigm shifts: Stephen Covey, *The 7 Habits of Highly Effective People*. Free Press, 1989.

On the complex neural connections underlying our habits: John Ratey, *A User's Guide to the Brain: Perception, Attention, and the Four Theaters of the Brain*. New York: Vintage, 2002.

Loehr and Schwartz's "manageable increments": James E. Loehr and Tony Schwartz, *The Power of Full Engagement*. New York: Simon & Schuster, 2013.

On the psychology of learning new behaviors: "Law of effect," Wikipedia.com.

Move Down the Path

An investigation of the "M&M rider" can be found at snopes.com: David Mikkelson, "Did Van Halen's Concert Contract Require the Removal of Brown M&Ms?" Jan. 19, 2001. Accessed March 26, 2020.

It's a Process

Teens mock a drowning man: Bopha Phorn, "Teens who mocked, filmed and failed to help drowning Florida man won't face charges." *ABC News* June 25, 2018. Accessed Mar. 26, 2020. https://abcnews.go.com

About the authors

Lance Tanaka

Asia Executive Resource Ltd.
Lance Tanaka Group
Managing Director
www.lancetanakagroup.com

Lance, a Japanese-American, was born, raised, and educated in the U.S. but has spent much of his professional life living and working in Fortune Global 500 companies throughout Asia such as Nike-Cole Haan and Pepsi-Cola.

As the founder of Asia Executive Resource Ltd (AER), a Lance Tanaka Group company, he provides executive coaching for the "best of the best," working with the leading multinational and local companies in their respective industries throughout Asia-Pacific. He is author of *Stories from the Top* and *Dream and Achieve*.

Wes Feltner Ph.D.

Lead Well Ministries Inc.
Founder and Director

Dr. Wes Feltner has spent the last 23 years in vocational ministry and leadership training and is founder of Lead Well Ministries. Dr. Feltner has a Ph.D. in Leadership, a M.Div. in Theology, and a B.A. in Organizational Communication. He is the author of *All Sides of the Savior: Exploring the Humanity of Jesus*.